# A FAMILY'S **daily** DEVOTIONALS for a *year*

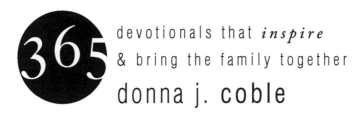 devotionals that *inspire* & bring the family together

donna j. coble

TATE PUBLISHING & *Enterprises*

*This book is dedicated*
*to three of my very best friends, my daughters,*
*Linda, Paula, and Suzanne.*

# Acknowledgments

I wish to thank my husband, Bob Coble, for his love, support and help, and to all of my family and friends for their encouragement.

Most of all, I thank God for His inspiration.

# Table of Contents

# Foreword

When I was asked to write the Foreword for Donna Coble's first book, "A Family's Daily Devotionals for a Year," many thoughts crossed my mind. Foremost was an overwhelming sense of " . . . not another brick onto the arms of an already stressed out workaholic." But quickly, I felt humbled to be presented with a tremendous honor. The honor is the privilege of giving you an introduction into the inspirational life of God's humble servant, Donna Coble, and her wonderful book of daily family devotions.

As a Naval Academy graduate and recently retired Naval Officer, I have had the exceptional experience of leading and been led by America's finest men and women. As a Christian, I have been given tremendous spiritual direction and examples of living an honorable spiritual life by many people, most importantly my mother and Mrs. Donna June Coble. You see, Mrs. Coble is the life-long partner of Lt Col. Robert N. Coble, USAF, Ret. Mrs. Coble was the steady "homeland" force that guided three young girls though multiple family moves and many long absences of a United States Air Force father. One of those young girls became my wife almost twenty-three years ago.

Very early in my experience with Donna, I came to realize she was a woman of extreme faith; faith honed through many personal hardships and a drive to be a person who lived a spiritually devoted life. Donna's steadfast love for her daughters and husband experienced many stressful days. She guided her children while their father flew combat missions in far off countries or awaited the Cold War call to arms no one desired to hear. Each of Donna's daughters followed in her footsteps. They became the guiding hand in families where the husband and father were most likely at sea defending our

Nation. Donna, again, provided love and leadership to her daughters, and by doing so, our country was greatly served.

She is a cancer survivor who now battles Parkinson's disease with tremendous vigor, courage, and grace.

Ten years ago, I discovered the cause of Donna's ability to remain a spiritual woman of grace who displays a personal love for Christ, no matter what comes her way. Donna absolutely is one who has turned her life over to Jesus. She lives her daily life to be an instrument of our Lord. She also has worked to bring the Lord into others' lives. Her formal studies at the Washington Theological Union led to her being designated as a Spiritual Director. She served in that position at her Maryland church for over ten years. Over those years, she led many small scripture study and prayer groups. She provided weekly, individual spiritual direction to numerous people. Donna personally opened my eyes to the power a simple, daily devotional reading and prayer time could have on my own life. Regardless of where in the world I was serving as a Naval Officer, or where I am today, I begin each day with a scripture reading and reflection. I owe Donna much for the daily devotion gift she provided.

"A Family's Daily Devotionals for a Year" provides a simple but tremendously powerful format for today's family to discover the power of conducting a daily devotional and discussion about our Lord's teaching and guidance. As you read each day's scripture verse, and a devotional exercise that brings into play the verse, you will come to understand what a gift this book is for you and your family. These easy to read devotions provide you an opportunity for discussion about using our Lord's teachings to help you tackle real life challenges. Our bookstores are full of self-help books by many famous, highly educated authors. Donna Coble's not that famous, yet. She's not the holder of many formal degrees. She just happens to be a lady who has weathered many personal storms, and did so while holding firm to God's great mysteries while experiencing the reign of Christ on earth. If there was a book titled "The XX Number of Habits of Highly Spiritual Families," I feel quite confident that the first habit of a highly spiritual family would be a daily reading from Donna's book.

Daniel G. Clague

# Introduction

One Sunday afternoon after attending church, Jim and Amanda Adams decided they wanted to bring the reading of scripture into the daily, ordinary flow of their family life.

At the evening meal, Jim and Amanda Adams discussed their desire for the reading of scripture with their children: Amy, Jake, Sara, Ted, and Sally.

At first, the children were not too sure if they wanted to read scripture on a daily basis. Amy and Jake were busy with their high school activities. Ted and Sara were in junior high school, and they did not think they were even old enough to understand scripture. They did not think that Sally, who was in kindergarten, could sit still through a reading of scripture. After the initial negative reactions, the Adams family decided to try the daily reading of scripture for a few days to see how they would like it.

The family decided the best time and place for the scripture reading would be at the dinner table after they finished eating. Jim and Amanda Adams said that they would take turns reading the scripture verses. The children would read also if they wanted to do so. Amanda Adams suggested the family close their eyes while listening to the scripture passage, and then spend time in silence reflecting on the passage. Anyone who wished to share could do so at the end of the silent reflection time. The family agreed, and this turned into a loved family tradition.

Let us now share the after dinner scripture readings and reflections with the "Adams Family."

# January

## January 1

John 15:12 "I demand that you love each other as much as I love you."

Amanda Adams wondered how she could love others as much as God loved her. How much did God love her, anyway? She had read that God is a compassionate God. Amanda wondered, "What does compassionate mean? Does it mean to suffer with? Does God suffer with us? Yes, God is with us, and he does suffer with us. It does not mean that God solves our problems, clears up our confusion, or answers our many questions, although he might do all of these things. What is important is that God loves us so much that he is willing to share our problems, our confusion, our questions, and our everyday, ordinary lives with us." Amanda then realized that showing love for each other is sharing with compassion the everyday, ordinary problems, confusion, and questions with one another; being with one another.

**How has God been a compassionate God in your life?**

**In what ways do you show compassion for others?**

## January 2

2 Peter 1:2–3 Do you want more and more of God's kindness and peace? Then learn to know him better and better. For as you know him

better, he will give you, through his great power, everything you need for living a truly good life.

Amy was experiencing difficulty in school. The problem was that she kept comparing herself with the other girls, and she felt she just did not measure up. "My hair is too straight, my legs are too fat, and my arms are too skinny. Where do I find God's kindness and peace at school? There is so much competition."

Then Amy realized that the more she learned about God and his love for her and for humanity, she then could stop comparing herself with others and begin feeling love for others instead. She was jealous, and that was making her into a petty person. She was grateful to God for the gifts he had given her as the unique human being God made her to be.

**Do you feel God's peace and kindness?**

**In what ways can you get to know God better?**

# January 3

Isaiah 55:1–3 Say there! Is anyone thirsty? Come and drink—even if you have no money. Come, take your choice of wine and milk—it is all free! Why spend your money on foodstuffs that do not give you strength? Why pay for groceries that do not do you any good? Listen and I will tell you where to get good food that fattens up the soul. Come to me with your ears wide open. Listen, for the life of your soul is at stake.

Jake was on the wrestling team at school, and he was trying to cut weight. He thought to himself, "Boy, I am always hungry. I never have enough money. I love junk food, but that just puts extra pounds on and really doesn't give the extra strength I need for team wrestling."

Then the thought of fattening up his soul came to him. "How

does a person fatten up his soul? He listens to God's word in scripture. What is more important? Is it worrying about gaining or losing weight for the wrestling team, or looking for the good food that fattens up my soul? I need to fatten up my soul."

**Do you worry about your body weight?**

**Is your soul in need of good nourishment?**

# January 4

Ezekiel 34:31 You are my flock, the sheep of my pasture. You are my men and I am your God so says the Lord.

Sara had gone on a field trip with her classmates to visit a farm. She saw cows, pigs, goats, and sheep. She tried to imagine God looking at a pasture filled with sheep. She remembered the sheep she saw looking so weak. They needed to be cared for and led into the right direction or they would end up lost.

"Does God lead us like sheep?" Sara wondered. "Yes, I guess he does. My religion teacher told our class that whenever we stray away, we need the Lord to guide us back to the flock."

Many times, her parents warned her not to do this or that, only to find that when she did not obey the warning, she got off track and away from the flock. That was always a lonely and scary experience for her.

**Do you feel like you are one of the sheep in the flock of God's pasture?**

**Do you feel that you can do nothing without God's help?**

# January 5

Romans 8:24–25 We are saved by trusting. And trusting means looking forward to getting something we don't yet have—for a man who already has something doesn't need to hope and trust that he will get it. But if we must keep trusting God for something that hasn't happened yet, it teaches us to wait patiently and confidently.

This reading was comforting to Jake. He was waiting to hear if the university he had his heart set on had accepted him. Each day was almost more than he could bear as he waited for the answer. "Can I really look forward to getting something I do not yet have, such as the acceptance to the university? Is this waiting teaching me patience and trust? What if I am not accepted? What will I do then? Perhaps being accepted by this university is not the best plan for me. Can I trust God's wisdom? Can I be confident that everything will be okay? Yes, I can." Jake then felt a wave of peace and quiet come over him.

**Do you trust God's wisdom?**

**Are you able to wait patiently and confidently for things that have not yet happened?**

# January 6

1 Peter 2: 1–3a So get rid of your feelings of hatred. Don't just pretend to be good! Be done with dishonesty and jealousy and talking about others behind their backs. Now that you realize how kind the Lord has been to you put away all evil, deception, envy, and fraud.

Amy was struggling with her jealousy of a friend at school she was working with on a project. Nancy was very popular and had everything that Amy wanted.

"Everyone likes Nancy except me. I almost hate her. She takes credit for much of the work that I am doing on the project. I can see the other side of Nancy that most people don't see. I ache to gossip about her and to tell everyone what Nancy is really like. God, please help me to feel compassion for Nancy. Help me to love and care about her. I don't want to hate her or feel jealousy and resentment toward her. I realize, Lord, that you are very kind to both Nancy and me. Help me put away these feelings of resentment and envy, Lord, in the name of Jesus Christ."

**Have you ever felt envy and resentment toward another person?**

**What affect did it have on your life?**

# January 7

Matthew 2:10–11 Their joy knew no bounds! Entering the house where the baby and Mother were, they threw themselves down before him, worshiping. Then they opened their presents and gave him gifts of gold, frankincense, and myrrh.

Sally loved this story about Baby Jesus. As her mother read this verse, Sally could picture the Wisemen coming to see Jesus. If only she could be there with them. In her imagination, she saw herself walking along with the Wisemen. They each carried a gift. What gift could she give Jesus?

"I know," Sally thought, "I will give him my favorite bear, Muffin. Jesus will love holding him in his arms for comfort. Muffin will give Jesus the love and comfort that I feel when I fall asleep at night holding Muffin in my arms. Jesus and I can be friends because we both love Muffin and each other."

**If you had been with the Wisemen when they visited Jesus, what gift would you have given to Jesus?**

**Do you and Jesus share and love the same things?**

# January 8

Mark 1:21–22 Jesus and his companions now arrived at the town of Capernaum and on Saturday morning went into the Jewish place of worship—the synagogue—where he preached. The congregation was surprised at his sermon because he spoke as an authority and didn't try to prove his points by quoting others—quite unlike what they were used to hearing.

Jim Adams had been dealing with a co-worker who was hard to communicate with because he always used a quote to prove his points. Quoting others got in the way of a two-way conversation that Jim wanted to share with this co-worker.

"Jesus spoke as an authority in the synagogue. Jesus was the authority. How I wish I could have been there to hear him in person," Jim thought to himself. "Yet, in listening to scripture, Jesus is still speaking across time to us. He still speaks as an authority, not having to try to prove his points by quoting others."

**Does Jesus speak to you across time as though you are sitting in the synagogue with the others in Capernaum?**

**What is Jesus telling you?**

# January 9

John 1:38–39 Jesus looked around and saw them following. "What do you want?" he asked them. "Sir," they replied, "where do you live?" "Come and see," he said. So they went with him to the place where he was staying.

Ted tried to imagine being with the two disciples following Jesus. What would he have answered when Jesus asked, "What do you want?" "What is it I do want?" thought Ted. "How would I have answered? I guess I would say that I am still in school, and I am in the process of learning about the world. However, I know I need to learn about you and your ways, so I can have a good foundation for learning about the world.

"Yes. Would I have followed when Jesus answered 'Come and see'? Gosh, I have a hard time keeping from yawning during church service. Does Jesus understand my yawning? I think he does. He was a little boy at one time. He would say, 'Let's be together and play ball, or share some fun hours of recreation.' I bet Jesus liked to play ball."

**What is your answer when Jesus asks, "What do you want?"**

**What is your answer when Jesus says, "Come follow me"?**


# January 10

John 5:19–20 Jesus replied, "The Son can do nothing by himself. He does only what he sees the Father doing and in the same way. For the Father loves the Son, and tells him everything he is doing."

As Jim Adams listened to Amanda read the above passage, he liked Jesus saying that he, the Son, can do nothing by himself. That he, the Son, does only what he sees the Father doing and in the same way.

Jim thought to himself, "How could I ever have thought I could live this life thinking I was in control of everything on my own? Here is Jesus saying that he, the Son, can do nothing by himself. We are all dependent on God, and we need to listen to what God is telling us through scripture, spiritual reading, church, and community. Father, I pray, that I will listen to what you are saying and that I do what you want me to do."

**What have been the results of your life when you felt that you were the only one in control?**

**Do you believe that you, like the Son, can do nothing by yourself?**

# January 11

Luke 10:21 Then He was filled with the joy of the Holy Spirit and said, "I praise you, O Father, Lord of heaven and earth, for hiding these things from the intellectuals and worldly wise and for revealing them to those who are as trusting as little children."

Amanda Adams often thought about trusting the Lord. Jesus wanted us to come to him as trusting little children. Amanda thought, "When we grow out of childhood, and with the loss of childhood comes the loss of basic trust. We become too smart for our own good in many situations. With worldly wisdom comes the loss of simplicity. Everything becomes so complicated. Many times I have felt so uneducated and pretty dumb; but there have been times when I have an inner knowing; and an inner wisdom that education and worldly wisdom could never teach me. Those times have been a pure gift from God, filling me with the trust of a child."

**Have you ever felt an inner knowing that worldly education could never teach you?**

**Do you trust in God like a little child?**

# January 12

Hebrews 1:1–2 Long ago God spoke in many different ways to our fathers through the prophets (in vision, dreams, and even face to face), telling them little by little about his plans. But now in these days he has spoken to us through his Son to whom he has given everything.

Amy thought that the Father loves us so much that he has used many ways to communicate with us—the ultimate way being through his Son, Jesus Christ.

"But," Amy thought, "Do I really pay any attention to what the Father is saying to me? I am involved with school, friendships, and thousands of distractions. I always feel that there will be time tomorrow to listen to God, but today I am too busy. Maybe I am busy, but I know that God is with me every moment. So in the center of my busy schedule, I can easily turn my mind over to God and acknowledge his presence."

**Are you awed by the many ways the Father has communicated with us—the ultimate being through his Son?**

**In what ways has God communicated with you?**

# January 13

1 John 4:7–8 Dear Friends let us practice loving each other, for love comes from God and those who are loving and kind show that they are the children of God, and that they are getting to know him better. But if a person isn't loving and kind, it shows that he doesn't know God—for God is love.

Sara asked herself, "Am I a person who is kind and loving to others? I try very hard to be. There is one boy in my class, though, who is nothing but a bully. It is hard to be kind and loving to him.

Mom tells me that he probably has a lot of hurt inside. She says that it would help not only him, but it would help me if I would pray for him each day. So, God, I put 'Harry the bully' into your care. Give me the patience to feel compassion for him, while at the same time not allowing him to bully me. I need your help, dear Father, to be a kind, loving person. I ask this in the name of your Son, Jesus Christ. Thank you, Father."

**Like Sara, have you ever run into a bully? How did you respond?**

**How can a person show love and kindness toward a bully and yet not allow that person to bully you?**

# January 14

Psalm 29:10–11 At the flood, the Lord showed his control of all creation. Now he continues to unveil his power. he will give his people strength. he will bless them with peace.

Amanda Adams remembered the flash flood that hit their house. The power of the water was awesome. It rushed through the house pushing the refrigerator from the kitchen and slamming it next to the living room front door. Fortunately, they were not at home when the flood hit.

"God, thank you for the strength you gave us. Thank you for the strength you gave our wonderful friends, who spent time helping us go through our muddy things. They gave us a place to stay. They cleaned up the items that we were able to save, also. Yes, Father, you did bless us with peace during those days of recovery. You blessed us with a loving community ready and willing to show us your love."

**Have there been times of trial when you have felt God's peace come to you through others?**

**Did you feel strong?**

# January 15

John 1:41–42 Andrew then went to find his brother, Peter, and told him, "We have found the Messiah!" And he brought Peter to meet Jesus. Jesus looked intently at Peter for a moment and then said, "You are Simon, John's son—but you shall be called Peter, the rock!"

Jake wondered, "What would Jesus call me? We guys at school have nicknames for each other. The guys call me 'Lefty' because I am left handed. What would Jesus call me? What are the things I do well? Let's see. I pitch a baseball really well. I am good at carving birds out of wood. I have even sold a few of the birds I have carved. I probably will go through life, though, never really knowing the name Jesus has given me, and that is okay. For right now, they call me 'Lefty' and 'Jake.' With God's help, I will do my best to do what God has planned for me."

**What name do you think Jesus would give you?**

**Are you content not knowing what the name is, and of not knowing what God wants you to do with your life?**

# January 16

Matthew 4:19 - 20 Jesus called out, "Come along with me and I will show you how to fish for the souls of men!" And they left their nets at once and went with him.

"Dear Jesus, there have been many times in my life when I would have gladly left my job and followed you," Jim Adams prayed. "I felt that life was so difficult and draining, any change would be a welcome relief. As it turned out, following you didn't mean for me to leave my difficult life and job. Rather, following you meant staying in my job and working through my difficult situation, trusting that all would work out okay. It meant trusting my life to your care. Perhaps following you by staying in a difficult situation is the harder thing to do. I trust you to give me the wisdom to know when I should stay and when I should make a change. Thank you, Lord."

**Have you ever been in a situation where you wished Jesus would walk up to you and say, "Follow me," and you could leave the situation behind?**

**What do you think Jesus means when he says, "Follow me"?**

# January 17

Luke 9:23 Then he said to all, "Anyone who wants to follow me must put aside his own desires and conveniences and carry his cross with him everyday and keep close to me!"

Amanda Adams felt a bit uncomfortable with this verse, saying to herself, "I used to think that following Jesus meant a person would have to find a cross to carry. Who would want to do that? As I get older, I realize that we don't have to look for crosses to carry. They find us. We are not to run away from the crosses, but instead face the reality of the crosses, pick them up, and carry with them the Lord's help. When we run away from the crosses of life, we then run into lots of problems; trying to escape from pain is no answer. Jesus, you have always been at my side as I have carried my crosses. Thank you, dear Lord."

**What crosses have you had to carry?**

**Did you want to run away from the crosses?**

# January 18

Matthew 10:42 "And if as my representative you give even a cup of cold water to a little child, you will surely be rewarded."

Sally pictured herself giving a cup of cold water to Julie, her little friend. She asked, "Mommie, what does it mean to give water to a little child and you will be rewarded? How will I be rewarded if I would give Julie a cup of water?"

"Oh, Sally, I imagine that Jesus is saying that when we show love, caring, and kindness to another person without thinking about being paid back, you will be rewarded, although you may not realize it. Being a representative of Jesus means giving love and compassion to each other without thought of a reward.'"

"You mean that if I give a cup of cold water to Julie, or to even a stranger because I love and care about that person, then Jesus will be proud of me, and that will be my reward, Mommie? Yes, Sally; it is something like that."

**What are your motives when you do something to help people?**

**Do you expect a reward, or are you helping because you have compassion in your heart?**

# January 19

Matthew 11:28–30 "Come to me and I will give you rest—all of you who work so hard beneath a heavy yoke. Wear my yoke—for it fits perfectly–and let me teach you; for I am gentle and humble and you shall find rest for your souls."

Jim Adams reflected, "This is my favorite verse. When I feel weary in body and soul, going to Jesus for rest always restores my soul. Listening to my breathing in the quiet of my heart makes me open to God's healing grace. I have learned that God works in his own way and in his own time. My weariness doesn't always pass as quickly as I would like it to. When I sit quietly in God's presence, rest does come. I find that God's yoke is light, but the yoke I allow myself can be very heavy. I can do nothing in this world without God's help. Thank you, Father, for your gentle and humble love. Amen."

**Can you go to God in prayer and find rest and peace?**

**Do you remember times when you have felt tired and drained? What did you do?**

# January 20

Matthew 19:25–26 "Then who in the world can be saved?" they asked. Jesus looked at them intently and said, "Humanly speaking, no one. But with God, everything is possible."

Amanda Adams reflected, "There was a time when I thought to be loved by God, I had to earn his love. I found that I wasn't strong enough to earn his love. No matter how hard I tried to do, the right thing, I generally messed up. I got to the point where I began to turn away from God because I could not measure up to what I thought he wanted me to be before he would love me. Then I learned about God's unconditional love. He wants me to be all I can be, but he loves me as I am. I learned that I couldn't save myself, but with God and his love, everything is possible. All I need to do is to be open to God's love. I need to receive his love with a listening heart. I want to become the person he wants me to be.

**Do you believe that God loves you unconditionally?**

**Are you becoming the person God wants you to be?**

# January 21

Psalm 40:1, 4 I waited patiently for God to help me; then he listened and heard my cry. Many blessings are given to those who trust the Lord.

Amy's eyes were swollen from crying. As she listened to her mother read these words, she pondered the events of the day. "I went to school this morning feeling so happy. Then I learned that my two best friends, Mary and Delores, were going to spend a week at the lake with Mary's family at their cabin. Mary didn't ask me to go. She asked Delores instead. I don't have any friends. I feel so left out. Why don't people like me? I am so lonely. God, do you hear my cry? How can you help me? Do I trust you to help me?"

As Amy sat in sad silence, a feeling of peace came over her. She knew this wasn't the end of the world. "I will make new friends. I am a likable person, and I like people. God loves me, and he is my best friend. Thank you, God, for your love. I do trust you."

**Do you trust God?**

**Do you remember a special time when he listened and heard your cry?**

# January 22

Isaiah 6:8 Then I heard the Lord asking, "Whom shall I send as a messenger to my people? Who will go?" And I said, "Lord, I'll go! Send me."

Jake wondered to himself, "Could I ever be a messenger to God's people? I really doubt it. It's all I can do to make up my mind what I want to major in when I go to college. If I were God's messenger, what would I say to his people? What does God say to me? Gee, I don't know. What does he want me to do with my life? Well, I guess he wants me to finish my schooling, to be a good person, to be responsible, to go to church, and to be kind to others. Most of all, I guess he wants me to love him and to realize that he loves me too. He wants me to love others, also. What did Jesus tell us to do? We are to love God with all of our heart, and to love our neighbor as we love ourselves. We are to love God and to love each other. Yes, God, I can be a messenger for you. I will tell everyone to love you and to love each other."

**Can you be a messenger to God's people?**

**What would your message be?**

# January 23

Luke 5:8,10 When Simon Peter realized what had happened, he fell to his knees before Jesus, and said, "Oh, sir, please leave us—I' m too much of a sinner for you to have around." Jesus replied, "Don't be afraid! From now on you'll be fishing for the souls of men!"

Ted was amazed! "St. Peter felt that he was too much of a sinner for Jesus to have around? Yeah, I guess all of us feel that we do many things that Jesus wouldn't like. I sure do. Just the other day at school, I tried cheating on a math test. It was the first time I ever tried cheating, and I was caught. Not only was it embarrassing, but also I really felt bad about it. It wasn't a good thing to do. Cheating is bad, and Jesus wouldn't like it. What would Jesus say to me? 'Don't be afraid! From now on, you'll be fishing for the souls of men.' Yeah, I guess he would say that to me. From my bad experience with the guilty feelings I have about cheating, I can discourage others from cheating. Sharing my experiences with others can be helpful to giving others the love and encouragement that Jesus would give."

**In what ways can you be fishing for the souls of men?**

**Do you feel that God forgives you for your sins? Do you forgive yourself?**

# January 24

Acts 9:3–5 As he was nearing Damascus on this mission, suddenly a brilliant light from heaven spotted down upon him! He fell to the ground and heard a voice saying to him, "Paul! Paul! Why are you persecuting me?" "Who is speaking, sir," Paul asked. And the voice replied, "I am Jesus, the one you are persecuting."

Jim Adams sat and tried to imagine himself in the scripture scene as Paul falls to the ground. It amazed Jim that Paul wanted to destroy the Christians, and was on his way to Damascus to persecute any believers he found. Then Paul was struck to the ground and was asked, "Why are you persecuting me?"

"What a shock that would be," Jim thought to himself. "It turned Paul's life completely around, and he became a leader in the early church. It just goes to show that no matter what our sin is, God can turn us completely around. We rarely if ever are blinded by light and fall to the ground; but nonetheless, God reaches out to us in many ways. It is up to us to choose to listen. The choice is ours."

**Have you ever had a flash of insight?**

**What did you choose to do with the insight?**

# January 25

1 Corinthians 1:28–29 He has chosen a plan despised by the world, counted as nothing at all, and used it to bring down to nothing those the world considers great, so that no one anywhere can ever brag in the presence of God.

Jake was at the stage of his life where he needed to make some decisions about what type of a person he wanted to be. "I am aware that there is a lot of competition in the world. Winning is everything. Get to the top and then brag about what a wonderful person you are. Don't commit to anything. Keep your options open. I am not comfortable with these ideas, though. I can't see why I can't live in the world, make a living, and even be successful without being selfish and climbing over everyone. God doesn't want us to live by the rules of the world. He loves us, and he wants us to love one another. I pray that I will always be humble; that I will have a good sense of myself, knowing I can do nothing without God. When I begin to believe I do everything without God's help, I become boastful and worldly.

**Have you ever felt like bragging when you did something you been proud of doing?**

**What were the results of your bragging?**

# January 26

2 Corinthians 4:8–9 We are pressed on every side by troubles, but not crushed and broken. We are perplexed because we don't know why things happen as they do, but we don't give up and quit. We are hunted down, but God never abandons us.

It had been a bad school year for Amy. She felt abandoned by her two girl friends. She had not made the pompon squad. She felt like a misfit. When she entered school every morning, there really wasn't anyone to talk to. She felt too shy to talk. Although she was a good student, she was even having trouble with a math course. She had become very sad and cried herself to sleep every night.

"Oh, God, I am perplexed because I don't know why this is all happening, but I do love going to church. I feel your peace there. I thank you for my family, too. I know that I will continue to feel sad for a while. I guess it is part of my growing up. But I won't give up and quit. Friends may abandon me, but I know you won't abandon me, God. Thank you."

**Have you ever feared being abandoned?**

**Are you able to get through the down times with a peace of mind, knowing that God will not abandon you?**

# January 27

John 21:17 Once more he asked him, "Simon, son of John, are you even my friend?" Peter was grieved at the way Jesus asked the question this third time. "Lord, you know my heart; you know I am," he said.

Sally wondered to herself, "If Jesus asked me if I was his friend, what would I say? Would Jesus care if I were his friend? After all, I am only a little girl. I know he is my friend and he loves me but does he want me to be his friend? Does he need friends? I guess he does. I never thought of that before. Jesus needs friendship just as I need friendship. I wonder if Jesus would like to go to the zoo with us tomorrow. I bet he would. Jesus, you are my very best friend, and I am your friend too. I love you so much, Jesus. Thank you."

**What is your answer when Jesus asks you "Are you my friend?"**

**How can you show Jesus that you are his friend?**

# January 28

Psalm 62:5–6 But I stand silently before the Lord, waiting for him to rescue me. For salvation comes from him alone. Yes, He alone is my rock, my rescuer, defense, and fortress—why then should I be tense with fear when troubles come?

As Amanda Adams read these lines aloud from scripture, she thought, "Why then should I be tense with fear when troubles come? Why can't I trust the Lord? I know he is my rock, but I have this bad habit of negative thinking. I am always looking on the bad side of things instead of seeing the good side. In my head, I know the Lord loves me and that everything will be okay, but in my heart, I am numb with fear when troubles come. I must admit, though, that most of the things I feared didn't happen, and everything did turn out okay. I found it was difficult getting through the troubles. But get through, I did. Oh, God, please help me to trust you in the deepest places of my heart. Amen."

**Is God your rock?**

**Do you trust him in the deepest places in your heart?**

# January 29

Genesis 1:1–3 When God began creating the heavens and the earth, the earth was at first a shapeless, chaotic mass, with the Spirit of God brooding over the dark vapors. Then God said, "Let there be light." And light appeared.

Jim Adams couldn't help but think to himself, "I wonder if as we humans struggle in this world, we remind God of the earth when it was a shapeless, chaotic mass. He is there brooding over us. Then he says, 'Let there be light' and we turn toward God and his light. We become beautiful, loving human beings, leaving behind our dark, shapeless, chaotic lives. Without God's light, we would be lost. Oh, God, how wonderful it would be to free of troubled days. I want to be free of struggling with the questions that can never be answered. We need to be satisfied with the mystery in itself. I thank you for your light of peace that comes to me even in the deepest darkness."

**Have you ever had a time in your life when you felt like a shapeless chaotic mass?**

**Did God's peace come to you? How?**

# January 30

John 15:1–3 "I am the true vine, and my Father is the Gardener. He lops off every branch that doesn't produce. And he prunes those branches that bear fruit for even larger crops. He has already tended you by pruning you back for greater strength and usefulness by means of the commands I gave you."

Amy felt like she was being pruned because of all the disappointments she had been experiencing. "How are these disappointments going to make me stronger, God? I am hurting so much. I feel bad about myself. I know I just plainly can't depend on other people to give me happiness; to make me feel good about myself. Oh, God, that's it, isn't it. My strength is coming from knowing that indeed, I cannot depend on other people to make me feel good about myself. Pruned, I must depend on you and find my sense of well-being from within myself—not in others. God, help me to learn how to find this life-giving strength within myself. Thank you."

**Have you ever felt like you were being pruned?**

**What strength did you receive from the pruning?**

# January 31

Acts 27: 22–25 "But cheer up! Not one of us will lose our lives, even though the skies will go down. For last night an angel of the God to whom I belong and whom I serve stood beside me and said, 'Don't be afraid, Paul—for you will surely stand trial before Caesar! What's more, God has granted your request and will save the lives of all those sailing with you.' "

Jake thought, "Boy, I've been in a fishing boat when suddenly a rain storm blew up. I was scared as we raced back to shore. Wow! Paul was brave. He had so much faith in God and believed that they all were going to be okay. Even if an angel of God appeared before me and told me that all would be well, would I believe the angel. Or would I discount that I had even heard an angel and continue to be afraid? How many times do I know that all will be well but continue to feel fear? That is the same as ignoring the angel, isn't it? I must be more like Paul and have faith."

**How many times have you ignored the voice of the angel saying deep within you, "All will be well"?**

**Do you have a deep faith that all will be well?**

# 2 February

## February 1

Acts 10:34–35 Then Peter replied, "I see very clearly that the Jews are not God's only favorites! In every nation, he has those who worship him, do good deeds, and are acceptable to him.

Sara's ears perked up at this reading. Earlier that day, one of Sara's classmates told Sara that she wasn't saved because she didn't go to the same church where her classmate went. "I don't understand. We both believe in you, God, but we worship you in different ways. It makes me feel uncomfortable to have someone think that I am not saved because I don't go to her church. I don't feel that way about them. I know that you love each one of us, and that each of us is unique. God, I pray that we become tolerant and feel compassion towards those who go to different churches or have a different devotion to you than we have. Help me to feel compassion towards my classmate."

**Are you accepting of other people and their belief systems?**

**Are you a compassionate person?**

## February 2

Luke 6:27–28 "Listen, all of you. Love your enemies. Do good to those who hate you. Pray for the happiness of those who curse you; implore God's blessing on those who hurt you."

Sara wondered, "God, how hard it is to love people who don't like you; people who hurt you. It's hard to pray for their happiness; like the kids at school who laugh at me because I can't throw a ball very well. When we choose teams, I am always the last one chosen. That hurts. I guess they really don't know any better, but it still hurts. Or like the kids at school who leave me out of their conversations, or the kids who like to tease me. But God, I know deep down I need to pray for these kids, that they receive your blessings and that they will be happy. I believe in turn, I will then be able to overlook the hurts, and I will feel peace and happiness. But God, it doesn't come naturally. I want to strike out at the kids. But with your help, I can let go of my hurt and anger. Thank you, God."

**When people hurt you, are you able to pray for them?**

**Why do you think praying for these hurtful people helps you?**

# February 3

Luke 8:46–47 But Jesus told him, "No, it was someone who deliberately touched me for I felt healing power go out from me." When the woman realized that Jesus knew, she began to tremble and fell to her knees before him and told why she had touched him and that now she was well.

Amy placed herself back into scripture. "I can see the woman reaching out to touch the edge of Jesus' robe. I can see the people crowding around Jesus and this woman. They want to be healed. The woman wanted to touch him. Jesus knew she touched him, and he turned and looked at her. I can see her falling to her knees. I can hear Jesus say 'Daughter, your faith has healed you. Go in peace.' How frightened the woman must have been. She probably didn't think Jesus would know she touched his robe since there was such a crowd. But he did know. He was kind and gentle to her, and her faith healed her. It just goes to show that Jesus knows when each of us touches the edge of his robe. Thank you for loving us. Amen."

**Have you ever reached out to touch the edge of Jesus robe?**

**What happened?**

# February 4

Psalm 37:4–5 Be delighted with the Lord. Then he will give you all your heart's desires. Commit everything you do to the Lord. Trust him to help you do it and he will.

Jake found this verse confusing. "What does it mean that if you are delighted with the Lord, he will give you all your heart's desires? So long as I am delighted with the Lord, will I get everything I want as a reward? No, I think not. The key phrase is 'to commit everything you do to the Lord.' If I commit everything I do to the Lord, then I will be trying to do his will—not my will. If I trust him to help me, then he will help me in his time and in his way. I need to give up control and allow God to manage my life. When I am allowing God to direct my life, my heart desires will be God's desires. I have a strong feeling that it is very hard to give up control and allow God to manage our lives. God, I need your help in helping me to trust. Thank you."

**Have you committed everything you do to the Lord?**

**If not, why not?**

# February 5

Luke 9:61–62 Another said, "Yes, Lord, I will come, but first let me ask permission of those at home." But Jesus told him, "Anyone who lets himself be distracted from the work I plan for him is not fit for the Kingdom of God."

Amanda Adams could hear herself saying to Jesus, "Yes, Lord, I will come, but first let me ask permission of those at home. How many times during my life have I made excuses, which kept me from following you, Lord? I always have one excuse or another. There are always distractions—always things that need to be done or taken care of. You, Lord, generally take a back seat. What am I going to do to put you first in my life? I must pray for your help. I'm not strong enough to keep from following my distractions instead of you. Perhaps I can place you in the proper place, which is at my side, and allow you to share my life. Then my life, with all of its distractions, will become a prayer. I do so love you, God."

**Is your life full of distractions that keep you away from the Lord?**

**Do you think you can become aware of God being with you every moment of your life, even with all of your distractions?**

# February 6

1 Kings 19:11–13 "Go out and stand before me on the mountain," the Lord told him. And as Elijah stood there the Lord passed by, and a mighty windstorm hit the mountain; it was such a terrible blast that the rocks were torn loose, but the Lord was not in the wind. After the wind, there was an earthquake, but the Lord was not in the earthquake. And after the earthquake, there was a fire, but the Lord was not in the fire. And after the fire, there was the sound of a gentle whisper. When Elijah heard it, he wrapped his face in his scarf and went out and stood at the entrance of the cave.

Sara loved this reading. "How many times we think we will find you, God, in windstorms, earthquakes, and fire because all three are powerful; yet, God, your coming as a sound of a gentle whisper is comforting. You are so powerful and so awesome that I could easily fear you. But knowing you so love, as to come to Elijah as a gentle whisper, brings me a feeling of trust. Trust knowing that you love us as a compassionate loving parent. You care about what happens to us."

**Can you recall a time when God came to you as a gentle whisper?**

**Do you think of God as a loving parent?**

# February 7

Philippians 1:19 I am going to keep on being glad, for I know that as you pray for me, and as the Holy Spirit helps me, this is all going to turn out for my good.

Jim Adams reflected, "Paul and Timothy wrote this letter to the Christians of the city of Philippi. Paul suffered much for getting out the good news to the early Christians. Could I be that strong? I think of life as it was then and as it is today. What am I doing to spread the word of the good news? I hope that I am a good example of God's love. I hope that I give compassion and encouragement to those around me. When there are bad times in life, am I still able to be compassionate and loving to others? Do I really believe that the down times really do turn out for my good? Well, I have found that I certainly do learn more from my down times or failures than my good times and successes. Yes, I am able to keep on being glad despite what is going on in my life. The good news is that you love me, God; I love you, and we all love each other."

**What have you learned from your successes?**

**What have you learned from failures? Did your failures turn out for your good?**

# February 8

1 Peter 5:7 Let him have all your worries and cares, for he is always thinking about you and watching everything that concerns you.

Amy found this verse to be encouraging. "I am always feeling anxious about everything. I become so tense that many times I find it hard to relax. I am afraid. Why am I afraid? I'm afraid that the people at school won't like me that I don't measure up. I am worried about what I am going to major in when I get to college. Lately, I have felt so self-conscious that I feel nervous when I am around people. Oh, God, to know that you are watching everything that concerns me tells me that you really do care about me. Can I let you have my worries and cares? Can I trust you to take good care of me? Perhaps if I can say at the start of each day, 'God, just for today, I give you all my worries and cares,' it will become a habit of turning my life over to you. Please allow me to surrender to your care."

**Are you able to turn your cares and worries over to the Lord?**

**If not, why not?**

# February 9

Luke 22:25–27 Jesus told them, "In this world the kings and great men order their slaves around and the slaves have no choice but to like it! But among you, the one who serves you best will be your leader. Out in the world the master sits at the table and is served by his servants. But not here! For I am your servant."

Jim Adams was struck by this verse. "Imagine Jesus saying 'I am your servant.' He didn't come to this world as a king or a master, ordering everyone around. Jesus came instead not to make slaves of us, but to free us. He came to free us from the enemies within us of envy, resentments, pride, and addictions. He frees us from all the other things that keep us away from God's love and peace. Jesus brought forgiveness that helps free us from these inner enemies by helping us forgive others as God forgives us. Oh, Jesus, thank you for serving us by freeing us from the inner torments. Help me to be open to your healing forgiveness."

**What are some of your inner enemies?**

**How has Jesus brought you from freedom from these enemies?**

# February 10

John 13:2–5 Jesus knew that the Father had given him everything and that he had come from God and would return to God. And how he loved his disciples! So he got up from the supper table, took off his robe, wrapped a towel around his loins, poured water into a basin and began to wash the disciples' feet and to wipe them with the towel he had around him.

This reading brought tears to Sara's eyes. "There you were, Jesus, knowing that you were going to die the next day, and at the Passover Meal you wanted to wash your disciples' feet. You loved them so much. You knew they didn't quite understand why everything seemed to be going the way it was. They thought you were going to save the Jews from the Romans. Instead, your kingdom was going to be the kingdom of God in our hearts, not an earthly kingdom. You are still washing our feet with your love and compassion. Jesus, I pray that I can be a friend to the kids at school like you are a friend to us."

**Do you feel that Jesus is washing your feet with his love and compassion?**

**Would you find it hard just as Peter did to have Jesus wash your feet? Peter said, "Master, you shouldn't be washing our feet like this!"**

# February 11

Psalm 112:7–8 He does not fear bad news, nor live in dread of what may happen. For he is settled in his mind that Jehovah will take care of him.

Amanda Adams remembered well when she lived in fear that something bad was going to happen. She was always waiting for the other shoe to drop. "Living like that was awful," Amanda mused. "I found I was afraid to be happy. If I felt happiness, then I would feel even worse, when the other shoe did drop. This type of thinking became a bad habit, and I was miserable most of the time. It was when the other shoe did drop that I found the pain was deep. But after a time, I realized that I was either going to sink or swim. I decided to swim and placed my torn life into God's hands. The pain was still there, but I knew that God was with me in the pain. Slowly but surely, the pain healed. The scar is still in my heart, but my life is stronger with God's loving presence."

**Have you ever lived in fear of what might happen?**

**Do you feel that God will be with you when bad times come?**

# February 12

1 Thessalonians 4:9 But concerning the pure brotherly love that there should be among God's people, I don't need to say very much, I'm sure! For God himself is teaching you to love one another.

Ted was studying current events in school. He could find few examples of brotherly love even among God's people. "Maybe the negative examples of human situations and wars are the only things that make the news," Ted thought to himself. "In fact, the news is down right depressing. Even history is filled with envy and hate. I guess it is part of the human condition. Is God teaching us to love one another? I wonder. Then I realize although God is teaching us to love, he gives us the choice. We can follow his will of loving others, or we can choose to follow our own will in not loving others. The ball is in our court. Lord, I pray to you to help me listen to your teachings about love. Help me to give to others the love and compassion that is called brotherly love."

**Are you listening to God as he teaches us about brotherly love?**

**In what ways can you show brotherly love to others?**

# February 13

1 Timothy 1:18–19 Now, Timothy, my son, here is my command to you: fight well in the Lord's battles, just as the Lord told us through his prophets that you would. Cling tightly to your faith in Christ and always keep your conscience clear, doing what you know is right.

Sally found it hard to understand many of the readings from scripture, but she did understand this one. "St. Paul sounds like Mom and Dad telling me to do what I know is right. The other day I dropped a glass, and it broke. I was afraid that Mom would be mad at me for dropping the glass, so I lied. I told her I didn't break it. She knew I was not telling the truth, and she became very stern with me. She said that she was not mad because the glass was broken, but she was because I told a lie. I felt terrible. I knew that telling a lie was wrong. Oh God, help me know right from wrong, and then help me do what is right."

**Do you think that St. Paul's advice to Timothy is good?**

**Do you believe that God will guide you in knowing right from wrong? What must you do?**

# February 14

Philippians 3:3 We Christians glory in what Christ Jesus has done for us and realize that we are helpless to save ourselves.

Amanda Adams surrendered her will to God a long time ago. "I used to believe that it was all up to me by doing good works and keeping all the rules. I did pretty well for quite a while. I did become somewhat self-righteous. After all, if I could choose to be a good person and keep all the rules, anyone else could, also. Then one day, I became burned out and very empty. There had to be more to life. After a time, I learned that the emptiness needed to be filled with a loving relationship with God. Doing good works and keeping the rules doesn't necessarily lead to a loving relationship with the Lord. However, having and nurturing a loving relationship with the Lord does lead to good works and keeping the rules. Now I am full instead of empty. Hopefully I am a kind, compassionate person instead of the self-righteous person I once was."

**Have you known self-righteous people?**

**Have you known compassionate people? What is the difference?**

# February 15

Ezekiel 33:32–33 You are very entertaining to them, like someone who sings lovely songs with a beautiful voice or plays well on an instrument. They hear what you say but don't pay any attention to it. But when all these terrible things happen to them—as they will—then they will know a prophet has been among them.

Amy was enjoying her youth group for teenagers at church. Their leader was fantastic. "I wonder though," Amy thought," how many of us are just being entertained by the fun, good music, and the good feelings we have? Do we really pay any attention to what is being said? How many of us believe that the good times will go on forever? What will happen to us when sorrow comes into our lives, when great temptations come about? Will we be able to draw on what we learned from the youth group meetings? Will we have a deep foundation of God's love? I pray that we do enjoy the group meetings, and that we take the message that is being given into our hearts."

**Do you feel that you have a good foundation of the Lord's love?**

**Have there been times when you have been able to draw on that foundation of God's love?**

# February 16

2 Timothy 1:13–14 Hold tightly to the pattern of truth I taught you, especially concerning the faith and love Christ Jesus offers you. Guard well the splendid, God given ability you received as a gift from the Holy Spirit who lives within you.

"I can't believe the Holy Spirit lives within me," Jake mused to himself. "I struggle everyday to do what is right. It would be so easy to go along with many of the guys at school. Heck, they have a blast. All is fun and games to them. Some of them have gotten into problems with drugs. Being messed up with drugs takes away any gifts that have been given to a person. The drug becomes the most important thing in the world to these guys. I guess the guys really aren't having a blast after all. It is all an illusion coming from a drug. I guess the Holy Spirit is living within me, because so far I haven't given in to the temptation these guys have. The Holy Spirit has given me the insight to choose right from wrong. Yes, God, I received from you the gift of knowing right from wrong."

**Do you remember the times you have been tempted and you had the insight to stay away from the temptation?**

**Do you feel that the Holy Spirit is within you?**

# February 17

Romans 6:6–7 Your old evil desires were nailed to the cross with him; that part of you that loves to sin was crushed and fatally wounded, so that your sin-loving body is no longer under sin's control, no longer needs to be a slave to sin; for when you are deadened to sin, you are freed from all its allure and its power over you.

"Yes, it is true," Jim Adams said to himself. "My old evil desires were nailed to the cross with Jesus. One by one, the Lord has helped me put away my bad habits. Giving up smoking is a good example of an evil desire of mine that was nailed to the cross with Jesus. Cigarettes controlled my life. I had gotten up to smoking three packs a day. It was terrible for my health and for my pocketbook as well. With God's help, my desire for cigarettes left me. Then I needed help with controlling my intake of food. I was eating everything in sight. That desire left me also! As days go by, I am freer from the allure of other sins, such as having a bad temper and being a perfectionist. One by one, I am being freed."

**Do you believe that your negative desires were nailed on the cross with Jesus?**

**Are you able to turn to Jesus for help?**

# February 18

Psalm 119:1–5 Happy are all who perfectly follow the laws of God. Happy are all who search for God, and always do his will, rejecting compromise with evil, and walking only in His paths. You have given us your laws to obey—oh, how I want to follow them consistently.

"I have problems staying out of trouble," Ted sadly thought to himself. "I have such a hot temper. It's not the anger that is wrong, but it's what I end up doing with my anger. If I could just learn to express my anger in a positive way instead of with my fists. Well, I know the laws of God do not encourage fistfights. Instead, Jesus said the greatest commandments are to love God and to love each other. Well, having fistfights with people I am mad at does not express any love that is for sure. I know I would be happy following God's laws. I do want to follow your wisdom, Lord. Please help me keep my cool and to express any anger I feel in a constructive way."

**Do you try to walk in God's path?**

**What are the results of compromising with evil?**

# February 19

Ephesians 6:10–11 Last of all I want to remind you that your strength must come from the Lord's mighty power within you. Put on all of God's armor so that you will be able to stand safe against all strategies and tricks of Satan.

The vision of wearing God's armor appealed to Ted. As he listened, he learned that the armor consisted of the strong belt of truth; the breastplate of God's approval; shoes to wear to speed you in preaching the Good News of peace with God; a shield to stop the arrows of Satan; a helmet of salvation; and the sword of the Spirit, which is God's work. "Wow, what a suit of armor. This sounds neat! The part I like best is carrying a sword. What does the sword represent? Oh yes, it is God's work. I guess that is right. If you learn what God's work is, you can use the knowledge as a sword to protect yourself against temptations of any kind, including my trouble with my hot temper. The most important thing to hang on to is that our strength comes from God's power inside us."

**Have you ever felt the need to put on the armor of God?**

**Do you feel the strength of God's power within you?**

# February 20

Hebrews 12:1 Let us strip off anything that slows us down or holds us back, and especially those sins that wrap themselves so tightly around our feet and trip us up; and let us run with patience the particular race that God has set before us.

"Oh, God, I have so many things that slow me down and hold me back in becoming the person I know you want me to be," prayed Amy. "My envy of my friends gets wrapped around my feet and trips me up. Envy prevents me from being the loving, compassionate person I know you want me to be. Can I be loving and compassionate to myself? Can I accept me the way I am instead of making myself miserable by being jealous of what other people have? Envy brings on anger, frustration, and a nature filled with a false pride. I am not free to be me. I am not free to run the race you have set before me, God. Please help heal me of this terrible sin of envy that is a part of me."

**What slows you down and trips you up in the race God has set before you?**

**What do you think God has planned for your life?**

# February 21

1 Peter 2:10 Once you were less than nothing; now you are God's own. Once you knew very little of God's kindness; now your very lives have changed by it.

"Yes, God's kindness is changing my life." Jim Adams answered to himself. "Although I always attended church, it took years for the message of God's kindness to reach into my heart. I went to church to fulfill some kind of duty. I didn't need God's kindness because everything was going along okay in my life. Then one day I asked, 'Is this all there is? I feel so empty!' Nothing was satisfying to me anymore. The things of the world didn't bring a very lasting happiness. Then one Sunday at church, I felt a strong desire to learn about God. I really wanted to read scripture. God's grace reached me, and my life completely changed to an overflowing abundance of God's kindness. How thankful I am for your love, God."

**Before you knew about God's kindness, did you feel like you were nothing?**

**Has your life been changed by God's kindness?**

# February 22

Philippians 3:13 No, dear brothers, I am still not all I should be, but I am bringing all my energies to bear on this one thing: Forgetting the past and looking forward to what lies ahead.

Amanda Adams shook her head in agreement that it is wise to let go of the past and to look forward to what lies ahead. "What is better yet is to live in the present moment. The past is gone, the future has not arrived yet,—all we have is the present moment. God is here with us in the present moment. I have learned to carry on a steady conversation with God. I feel God's grace of his moment-by-moment presence. What a gift of God's love. There are times of course that God seems far away. When that happens, my having over done it, not eating properly, and not getting enough rest, usually causes it. I am not all I should be, either, but I am on the journey toward all I will be with God's grace.

**Are you able to let go of the past?**

**Are you able to live in the present moment?**


# February 23

Matthew 23:11–12 "The more lowly your service to others, the greater you are. To be the greatest, be a servant. But those who think themselves great shall be disappointed and humbled; and those who humble themselves shall be exalted."

Amy could not help but to think of a classmate, Nan, who was president of their class and a straight-A student. Nan had everything in the world. Her parents had money, and were able to give Nan a car and a beautiful wardrobe. There was only one problem, and a serious one. Nan was a self-centered person who looked down her nose at people. "I've tried to get to know Nan, but she only runs around with people who she thinks can do something for her. I sometimes wonder if Nan really knows who she is. I wonder if she is happy. The only thing she has are things the world holds important which isn't very lasting. I did feel jealous of Nan until I learned that I really am happy to be who I am. I can trust God to help me be the person he wants me to be. I don't have to be what the world wants me to be."

**Have you seen people who have had the things the world offers become empty and depressed?**

**What does bring lasting happiness?**

# February 24

Matthew 7:13 "Heaven can be entered only through the narrow gate! The highway to hell is broad, and its gate is wide enough for all the multitudes that choose its easy way. But the Gateway to Life is small, and the road is narrow and only a few ever find it."

"The Gateway to Life is small," Jim Adams reflected. "The Gateway to Life is through a belief in the Lord. However, the highway to Hell is very wide and very easy to find. Just follow what is important to the world and very quickly, a person can find himself in the fast lane. Many people living in this age, they ignore the good news of the Gospel. Then these very people wonder why they feel so empty, why the 'good times' do not last. They wonder why there is so much suffering in the world. Why don't they feel peace? Where is God, they shout! Peace of a man's soul comes only through entering that narrow Gateway of Life by desiring and seeking a relationship with the Lord."

**Have you been running after the things of the world?**

**Have you been seeking a relationship with the Lord?**

# February 25

Psalm 37:4–5 Be delighted with the Lord. Then he will give you all your heart's desires. Commit everything you do to the Lord. Trust him to help you do it and he will.

Jake was dreading finals this semester. He brooded to himself, "I have been having trouble this semester with my grades. I have been spending too much time hanging out with the guys and not enough time cracking the books. What does it mean to be delighted with the Lord? I cannot see him or really hang out with him as I do with the guys. What are my heart's desires? Well, I want to do well in school and do well on my finals. Does hanging out with the guys help reach my goals? No. Would hanging out with the Lord help me reach my goals? Well, it would sure help. First, I would have to find out if my goals and the Lord's goals for me are one in the same. I feel they are, so God, I will trust you to help me crack the books and turn to you for your guidance. Each day I will turn my life over to you."

**Are you delighted with the Lord? What does being delighted with the Lord mean to you?**

**Do you commit everything you do to the Lord? If not, why not?**

# February 26

John 10:9–10 "Yes, I am the Gate. Those who come in by way of the Gate will be saved and will go in and out and find green pastures. The thief's purpose is to steal, kill and destroy. My purpose is to give life in all its fullness."

Amanda Adams turned over the scripture she was reading in her mind. "Jesus is saying that his purpose is to give life in all its fullness. How true. What peace we feel when we know we love God with all of our hearts, accepting his forgiveness, and in turn forgiving ourselves and others. Life is full when with the Lord's help. We let go of all of our hurts, angers, and jealousies. We stop clinging to favorite attachments. Most of all, we give control of our life over to God. Who is the thief? The thief who steals, kills, and destroys us is our useless worries and anxieties. Self-pity, negative thinking, and useless guilt take us away from God's love and care. Yes, the Lord is the Gate. He is our Good Shepherd who brings us love and peace."

**What is the name of the thief that takes away your peace of mind?**

**In what ways has the Lord been the Good Shepherd in your life?**

# February 27

Luke 15:1–2 Dishonest tax collectors and other notorious sinners often came to listen to Jesus' sermons; but this caused complaints from the Jewish religious leaders and the experts on Jewish law because He was associating with such despicable people—even eating with them!

Sara felt confused. "Mom won't allow me to be around Lottie because she has been caught shoplifting at the shopping center. Moreover, Lottie is always in some kind of trouble. I guess Mom is afraid that Lottie will be a bad influence on me, and maybe she would be. I know people would judge me in a bad light if I hung out with her. Mom did tell me, though, that I should care about what happens to Lottie and feel compassion for her. I need to love and pray for her even though I don't like what she is doing. Would Jesus hang out with Lottie? Yes, he would. He would not like what she was doing, but he loves her. If she will choose to listen to him and accept his love, she can heal. It is between the Lord and Lottie. I put her into your care."

**Have you ever thought to yourself, "There but for the grace of God go I?"**

**Why is having a close relationship with the Lord so very important?**

# February 28

Psalm 121:1–4 Shall I look to the mountain gods for help? No! My help is from Jehovah who made the mountains! And the heavens too! He will never let me stumble, slip or fall. For he is always watching and never sleeping.

Sally had seen a movie on television that showed a monster that really scared her. "I'm having nightmares about the monster. I know there is nothing to be afraid of, but deep inside, I feel so scared. Last night I screamed out in my sleep. Mom and Dad came into my room and reassured me that I was safe, so I was able to fall back to sleep. They told me that God was at my side watching over me and protecting me, keeping me safe. This morning we talked about the monster. I realized that the movie was the cause of my bad dreams. God, I trust you to be at my side at all times. You will keep me safe from harm. I know now that I can sleep in peace because you are with me. You will never let me slip, stumble, or fall."

**What monsters have there been in your life?**

**Do you believe that God is at your side at all times?**

# 3 March

## March 1

Revelation 22:3–5 There shall be nothing in the city which is evil; for the throne of God and of the Lamb will be there and his servants will worship him. And they shall see his face; and his name shall be written on their foreheads. And there will be no night there—no need for lamps or sun—for the Lord God will be their light, and they shall reign forever and ever.

"What beautiful words," Amanda Adams whispered to herself. "A time will come when there will be no evil. There will be no night. God will be the light. Life is such a mystery. For many years, I asked so many whys. I raged at God for all the suffering in the world. How could he treat humans so badly? Why did he allow evil to exist? I asked him many questions and found no answers. Then despair set in, and I felt so drained. Slowly the light of God came into me, lighting up the darkness. I became content to live with the questions, accepting the mystery. I accepted God's love instead of heaping blame on God, who brings nothing but goodness and peace to the world. Thank you for healing my despair. Amen."

**Have you ever felt despair?**

**Are you able to accept the mysteries?**

# March 2

Jeremiah 31:28–30 In the past I painstakingly destroyed the nation, but now I will carefully build it up. The people shall no longer quote this proverb—"Children pay for their fathers' sins. For everyone shall die for his own sins."

"Interesting," Jim Adams thought to himself. "Our society is quick to point fingers, trying to find someone or something to blame. If children grow to be criminals, the parents, poverty, society, and prejudice are to blame. Rarely is the blame put on the person himself who has turned into the criminal. How many trials take place where the defense lawyer will put the blame on the victim instead of the criminal? Our society is always looking for the quick fix, and pointing fingers can feel like a solution. We would be better off if instead of looking outside ourselves, we would instead look inward and face whatever is inside us. We each are responsible for our own behavior. Taking on responsibility for ourselves can enable us to ask for God's help, and if need be, for his forgiveness and healing."

**In what ways do you see society pointing fingers?**

**Are you able to accept responsibility for your own life?**

# March 3

Psalm 103:13–16 He is like a father to us, tender and sympathetic to those who reverence him. For he knows we are but dust, and that our days are few and brief, like grass, like flowers, blown by the wind and gone forever.

During a conversation Amy had with her grandmother about life, her grandmother said the older she got, the faster time went by. For Amy, time seemed to stand still. "I can hardly wait until I get the braces off my teeth, until I get my driver's license, until I finally grow up, and until I can make my own decisions without Mom and Dad bossing me around. Then the scripture reading says that God is like a father to us, tender and sympathetic to those who respect and honor him. Therefore, I guess Mom and Dad are not bossing me around, but are trying to guide me and to be tender and sympathetic. They want what is best for me. They know that soon enough I will be grown up. Instead of freedom, I will find the responsibilities of adulthood facing me. The most important thing on earth is our love of God and for each other. Life is too short for anything else."

**Do you think of God as a tender and sympathetic Father?**

**How are you living your life?**

# March 4

Matthew 18:2–3 Jesus called a small child over to him and set the little fellow down among them and said, "Unless you turn to God from your sins and become as little children, you will never get into the Kingdom of Heaven."

Ted could not believe what he heard. "Jesus actually said that unless we become like little children, we will never get into the kingdom of heaven? Who wants to be like Sally? She is a brat. She gets into my things. She is a pest. I love her because she is my sister, but boy, I do not like some of the things she does. Yet, I have to admit there are times when I know she really looks up to me. She wants to be around me all the time, and she trusts me. She is fun loving and warm, and a joy when she is behaving. I guess Jesus is saying that when we are like little children, we are innocent, trusting, and filled with love. However, I am going to have to think about this a bit more. Here I am trying to act as if I am grown up, and I am told by Jesus that we should become like little children. It is confusing. Help me to understand your concept of being child-like. Thank you."

**What is there about being an adult who could keep us out of the kingdom of heaven?**

**Do you have the childlike qualities of faith, trust, and love of the Lord?**

# March 5

Matthew 15:10–11 Then Jesus called to the crowds and said, "Listen to what I say and try to understand: You aren't made unholy by eating non-kosher food! It is what you say and think that makes you unclean."

Sara remembered, "Mom told me about all the laws that the Jewish people had, and that they obeyed these laws to the letter. I guess Jesus had many problems with many of the Jewish leaders because they didn't think Jesus followed some of the laws, like Jesus healing people on the Sabbath. I wonder what Jesus means when he says it's what you say and think that makes you unclean. Suppose when I am at school and I follow all of the school's regulations and obey the school's laws, would that make me a good person? Yes, it would. Okay then, if I follow the school's laws but feel hatred in my heart, then I am not a good person. If I do not feel love towards God, towards others, and towards myself, keeping all the laws in the world will not make me a good person. God, help me to keep my heart loving."

**Have there been times when you have been a person who follows the laws, yet you said and did things that brought pain to others?**

**What does Jesus mean when he says that it is what you think that can make you unclean?**

# March 6

Mark 10:45 "For even I, the Messiah, am not here to be served, but to help others, and to give my life as a ransom for many."

This verse hit Jake's mind with a jolt. "Wow! Here is the Son of God, who came to earth to establish the kingdom of God, and he is saying he did not come to earth to be served, but to help others and to give his life up as a ransom. Jesus loves us that much he give up his life for us. God his Father sent Jesus to help us and die for us. What love! When the world thinks of someone being a king, it thinks of power. A king has the authority to insist that people be his servants. However, we have a kingdom of God where the one with the power gives his people the freedom of choice. It is the power to help people be all they can be. God's power doesn't want to possess people; he wants to love them. He wants to have relationship with people only if they allow a relationship to happen. Wow!"

**How does Jesus help you in your day-to-day living?**

**Do you feel that you have the kingdom of God in your heart?**


# March 7

Matthew 5:6 Happy are those who long to be just and good, for they shall be completely satisfied.

Sara wondered to herself, "Do I long to be just and good? Well, I want to be a good person. Most of all, I do not want to judge others, but dear God, I seem to always goof up. Like the other day, Jill, a new girl at school, was thought to be a snob. I tried to get acquainted with her. When she did not say much, I judged her to be conceited. I thought she felt she was just too good for us. Well, I was wrong. The next day I went to the rest room and found Jill crying. I felt awful. I asked her what was wrong, and she told me how lonesome she was for her old friends, home, and school. She said she was a very shy person and found it hard to talk to people she did not know. She was not a snob at all. I had judged her all wrong, and I did not show her any loving understanding by snapping to quick conclusions about her. God, I do long to be just and good. I know you will help me."

**Do you judge people or do you accept people as they are?**

**Do you long to be good and just?**

# March 8

Matthew 5:13 You are the world's seasoning, to make it tolerable. If you lose your flavor, what will happen to the world?

Sara thought carefully about the verse as her mother read it. "Just the other day, I became very angry on our way to visit the zoo. I do not know why, but Ted and Sally were sitting in the back seat of the car singing stupid songs that got on my nerves. I asked them to be quiet, and then I started screaming for them to stop singing, so they stopped. Mom and Dad looked around at me, and I just did not care. I did not want to go to the zoo. I had wanted to go to the circus with my girlfriend's family instead of going to the zoo. Dad parked the car and we began walking all over the place. I got more and more irritable. Before long, the day was ruined for everyone because of my selfish mood. I affected everyone's mood. That day I lost my flavor. Each of us touches everyone who is around us. I guess it is best to have the flavor to make the world tolerable of those around us."

**Have you ever lost your flavoring?**

**What happened to the world around you?**

# March 9

Matthew 6:34 "So don't be anxious about tomorrow. God will take care of your tomorrow too. Live one day at a time."

Amy felt that this was a very sensible thing to take to heart. "I worry about everything—my grades, my after school job. Will I be accepted by the college of my choice? What should I major in? Mom says I take life too seriously. She says I should turn to you, God, to give me guidance. She said to do the best I can and leave the rest up to you, God. I know I need to live one day at a time. I do need to lighten up a little. Too many of my friends are not serious enough, and I sometimes envy their lack of concern about grades. I do not know why I have really liked school and have been anxious about it, too. God, will you really take care of my tomorrow, too? I think I have gotten into a bad habit of worrying about everything. I need to turn my useless anxiety and worries over to you. Please help me to let go of this very bad habit of mine."

**Do you worry about tomorrow?**

**What do you do with the present moment? Do you worry about the future or the past instead?**

# March 10

Psalm 2:1 What fools the nations are to rage against the Lord! How strange that man should try to outwit God!

"That's true," Amy agreed in her mind. She was studying Ancient History that year at school. "History tells stories of jealousy, greed, pride, and power that make people and therefore nations into fools. These negative qualities bring suffering to humans. Since the beginning, humankind has tried to outwit God. Each generation believes it knows more than God does, and the results are sad. Each generation has to learn the hard way that God is supreme. When we follow God's will of loving him and loving our neighbor, we find the peace and wholeness he wants of us to have. God is the answer to the seeking we all do for self-fulfillment. Thank you, God, for loving us and wanting us to be whole people filled with love and compassion."

**What are some of the things you have done trying to outwit God?**

**What are some examples from history of nations trying to outwit God?**

# March 11

Isaiah 6:8 Then I heard the Lord asking, "Whom shall I send as a messenger to my people? Who will go?" And I said, "Lord, I'll go! Send me."

"Wow!" exclaimed Jake quietly. "I wonder what I would say if God asked for volunteers to take his message to his people. I am afraid I would not have much courage. Most of the prophets back in those days were not very popular. In fact, most prophets today are not very popular. People do not want to hear their message because the message from the Lord always calls for change, and no one likes change. Next year when I graduate from high school will be cause for a change. I have mixed emotions about leaving all my friends and my familiar routine of high school for the responsibilities of beginning a new stage of life. I am comfortable where I am right now, but I cannot hang on to this moment. Time marches on, and with God's help, I will grow through the changes."

**What changes in your life cause the most growth?**

**How would you answer if God called on you to deliver his message to his people?**

# March 12

Luke 9:58 But Jesus replied, "Remember, I don't even own a place to lay my head. Foxes have dens to live in, and birds have nest, but I, the Messiah, have no earthly home at all."

"But I, the Messiah, have no earthly home at all" ran over and over through Jim Adams's mind. "I never thought about Jesus not owning a place to lay his head. Jesus lived in the world, but was not of the world. How many times in my life have I turned completely away from the Lord while striving to find my place in the world, collecting possessions, honors, and pleasures? Too many times, I am sorry to say, which always brought me stress, anxiety, and frustration. When the stress became too much, I would then realize that my life was out of balance. I indeed needed the Lord in my life reminding me that I live in the world. The things of the world are not that important. Loving God and loving others is what is important. This brings peace to the soul."

**How many times have you turned away from the Lord when striving for worldly possessions, such as honors, status, pleasures, and goods?**

**What were the results?**

# March 13

Acts 9:15 But the Lord said, "Go and do what I say, for Paul is my chosen instrument to take my message to the nations and before kings, as well as to the people of Israel."

"Gosh, if I remember right," Ted thought looking back to what he learned in religion class, "many of the believers were afraid of Paul because he had persecuted the followers of Jesus in Jerusalem. They wondered if he was faking the new belief he had in Jesus. It is amazing to see an example of how a person can change. Here, Paul spreads the good news of Jesus not only to the Jews but to the other people in the world as well. God works in strange ways. My religion teacher said that we each are special. No two of us are alike. God reaches us in different ways. For St. Paul, it was being knocked to the ground and hearing Jesus speak to him. For most of us, though, it is a slow process of insights about God. Thank you, Lord, for making each of us different; I like that, God."

**What happened that made you aware that God was working in your life?**

**Was it a sudden insight or was it a slow process for you?**

# March 14

Colossians 1:29 This is my work, and I can do it only because Christ's mighty energy is at work within me.

"How true," Amanda Adams whispered to herself. "I've been asked where I muster up the extra energy to work, raise a family, and to volunteer at church. I sometimes wonder about it myself. God has given me the energy I need to take care of the work I need to do. The first thing each morning, I dedicate the day to the Lord, asking him for his guidance. I keep things in perspective that way, so I am not carried away in anxiety and worry. I do what I feel God wants me to do and then leave the rest in his loving hands. I know one thing for sure; I cannot do a thing without his help. Knowing that he and I are sharing the workload of the day gives me the energy I need. Thank you, Lord, for helping me and being with me every minute of my life."

**Where do you get your energy for living each day?**

**Do you feel that God is with you at all times?**

# March 15

Galatians 1:10 You can see that I am not trying to please you by sweet talk and flattery; no, I am trying to please God. If I were still trying to please men, I could not be Christ's servant.

Amy thought back to the slumber party she went to the night before. She came home that morning feeling a bit guilty. "Here, St. Paul is saying that he can't be the servant of Christ if he is trying to please the people he is teaching with sweet talk and flattery. So what did I do last night? I went out of my way to compliment and be part of the group, even when they started talking about my friend, Lottie, behind her back. I did not say one word to defend her. I did not tell them that I thought they were being unkind and that they should not tear her down. That it is not good to judge someone, laugh and make fun of someone. In addition, I went along with it. I was trying to please that group at the expense of Lottie. I am not a servant of God when I act as I did last night. God, I am so sorry."

**Do you ever try to fit in and be a part of a group at the expense of others?**

**Do you feel that you are a servant of Christ?**

# March 16

2 Peter 1:11 And God will open wide the gates of heaven for you to enter into the eternal kingdom of our Lord and Savior, Jesus Christ.

Jim Adams reflected, "I can relate to Peter so well. He struggled in trying to understand what Jesus was all about. I, too, have struggled with my thoughts about who Jesus is and what the 'good news' is all about There is so much I don't understand and will never understand. Nor am I expected to understand. What I need to do is accept the mystery of it all. God wants me to become a whole person and wants nothing more than my good. God wants me to have a relationship with him, accepting all the mystery of the Lord's kingdom. Peter came to the place in his life where he accepted the mystery and the "good news." Then he went out to preach the message. He knew Jesus firsthand, and he too had to go through the process of faith—just as I have had to go through the process of faith.

**Can you relate to Peter?**

**Can you accept the mystery?**

# March 17

Psalm 130:1 O Lord, from the depths of despair I cry for your help. "Hear me! Answer! Help me!"

Amy brooded, "God, I do ask for your help. I feel so listless, so weary, so depressed. Joy has gone out of my life. Everything seems so pointless. I just do not fit in anywhere at school. I do not fit in with my friends. I do not feel good about myself at all. I guess Mrs. Lars cutting down my theme paper today in front of everyone in English class was just too much. The last straw was spending the last few days of doing nothing right. I am beginning to feel so self-conscious. My mind just goes blank. God, please help me realize that you do love me and that you are at my side. You feel bad right along with me when people cut me down. I do so need your help and guidance in not allowing 'me' to put myself down. Please help me to be able to accept criticism in a positive way. Thank you, Lord."

**Are you able to accept criticism in a positive way?**

**Are you able to accept God's love and guidance?**

# March 18

John 13:14 "And since I, the Lord and teacher, have washed your feet, you ought to wash each other's feet."

Jake thought, "You know, it's easy to love Jesus by praying and going to church. What is much harder to realize is that Jesus loves me and has indeed washed my feet by his life, death, and resurrection. What then is expected out of me is to love and accept others, and to wash their feet just as Jesus has washed my feet? There are some guys at school I just plain don't like. Man, if I am asked to wash their feet, I want to refuse. Jesus gives a tough message to us. I guess some people are hard to care about, but we are asked to care. Sure, we may not like what they do, but Jesus asks us to care about those people. We need to pray for them, to want the best for them, and to wash their feet. Wow! Jesus, please help me to be like you in your compassion and love."

**What does washing the feet of others mean to you?**

**Can you give an example in your life when you have had to give love and compassion to those you had a hard time liking?**

# March 19

Matthew 10:16 "I am sending you out as sheep among wolves. Be as wary as serpents and harmless as doves."

"The world is indeed full of wolves," mused Amanda Adams. "Here we are, raising these five children, trying to teach them to be loving, responsible human beings living in a world like sheep among wolves. It is so hard to get the message across to them that they should be wary as serpents and harmless as doves. It takes courage, an inner knowledge, and trust. Compassion coming from your love,

Lord, for them to live as responsible human beings. We want the children to love and trust others. We tell them to be aware of the temptations that come from the world and from others. We may not like what others do, but we still care about them and pray for them. Help us, God. Amen."

**What does living as sheep among wolves mean to you?**

**In what ways can a person be as wary as a serpent and as harmless as a dove?**

# March 20

John 15:15 "I no longer call you slaves, for a master doesn't confide in his slaves; now you are my friends, proved by the fact that I have told you everything the Father told me."

Sara's religion teacher at church talked about this verse from scripture that previous Sunday. "I really don't know what scripture is trying to tell me so much of the time," thought Sara. "I have so much to learn. I do know that Jesus loves us so much that he wants to share with us all the things that he says His Father in Heaven told him. We are his friends, he loves us, and he wants us to love him. Also, Jesus wants us to love each other just as he loves us. It's hard to have a friendship with someone I can't see. It's easy to be friends with my best friend, Sue, because I can see her. Jesus, I pray that you will guide me and show me how to have a friendship with you."

**In what ways are you able to express your friendship with the Lord?**

**At what point in your life did that relationship with the Lord begin?**

# March 21

Acts 6:12–13 This accusation roused the crowds to fury against Stephen, and the Jewish leaders arrested him and brought him before the council. The lying witnesses testified again that Stephen was constantly speaking against the Temple and against the laws of Moses.

"Dad said that Stephen was later stoned to death because of these lies," remembered Ted. "Wow! It is awful to have lies told about you. Last week at school, some of the guys told lies about me. They told Mrs. Bell that I was the one who hid the snake she found in the bottom drawer of her desk. After letting out a couple of screams when she opened her drawer, these guys pointed at me and said I was the one who put the snake in her drawer. I don't know if Mrs. Bell believed me when I told her that I wasn't the one who did it, and that I didn't know who did it, either. So I am at the mercy of Mrs. Bell's faith in me as a person who tries to do what is right. At least I know that I won't be stoned like Stephen was. Lord, please help me to forgive the guys who falsely accused me of something I didn't do."

**Have you ever been accused of something you didn't do?**

**What was your reaction?**

# March 22

James 1:13 And remember when someone wants to do wrong, it is never God who is tempting him, for God never wants to do wrong and never tempts anyone else to do it.

"That's what Mom told me the other day when I asked her if God was the one who sent temptations to test us. That was what our neighbor, Mrs. Tillie, said," Amy thought to herself. "So that is what St. James is saying also. That does make sense. God never wants to do wrong, so of course he wouldn't want to tempt anyone else to do wrong. Mom told me to pray hard for God's help in overcoming temptations. The world and life in general are full of temptations, Mom said. That is a part of what she called the human condition. Life is a struggle to do what is right. We can't succeed with overcoming a temptation all on our own. We need God's grace-filled guidance. God, there is so much to learn. Help me to not give in to the temptations that are apart of being human and living in this world."

**In what ways do you overcome temptation?**

**What temptations do you struggle with?**

# March 23

1 Peter 4:19 So if you are suffering according to God's will, keep on doing what is right and trust yourself to the God who made you, for he will never fail you.

This hit home with Jake. He had been struggling with wanting to be with the guys at school. But lately, the guys had been getting together just to get drunk. The drinking was getting pretty heavy. "God, I just don't know what to do anymore. I know that I don't want to get smashed. It is wrong. It affects my attitude towards everything, and it is a negative attitude at that. I guess I am going to have to find some new friends. I pray that these guys will soon realize that God doesn't want them to get drunk. I will trust you to take care of me, God. You guide me in knowing how to keep a good balance between work and recreation. Heavy drinking definitely is not the right kind of recreation. Thank you, God. I know you will never fail me. Amen."

**Have you ever felt suffering for doing what you felt was the right thing to do?**

**How did you feel? Did you ask for God's help?**

# March 24

Psalm 105:4 Search for him and for his strength and keep on searching!

Amanda Adams remembered, "Oh, all those days not too long ago, God felt so far away. I felt so empty despite the fact that everything was going along okay. I remember trying to pray, and I felt like I was just going through the motions. These were painful days of feeling abandoned by God. I am so glad I still felt the desire to want to go through the motions despite the way I felt. I wanted to be faithful to God. I wanted his strength to lead me on my daily walk. I began searching for him by reading books written about spirituality and the scripture, and I went to church and prayed. Then one day I began to feel God's presence again in my life. I realized how much I had learned and had grown during this time of searching. God's grace had been with me the whole time. Thank you, Lord."

**What do you do during those times when God seems so far away?**

**In what ways have you grown during those times of searching?**


# March 25

Psalm 63:1 O God, my God! How I search for you! How I thirst for you in this parched and weary land where there is no water. How I long to find you.

Amanda Adams remembered the time when she felt a feeling of despair that she did not understand. "Yes, God, it was then that I realized that the world is a parched and weary land where there is no water. It was a time when I faced the fact that no one person and no one thing in this world could completely fill up that empty place deep inside my soul. It was then I realized that only you could fill up the longing we humans feel. Then I began that search to find you, only to realize that you had been in my heart the whole time.

You were only waiting for me to notice you. It was only through the pain of my despair that I noticed you. I will spend the rest of my life building a relationship with you. Thank you for your loving grace."

**Has there been a time when you felt the world was a parched and weary land where there wasn't any water?**

**Are you longing to find God? Is He already there, waiting for you to notice him?**

# March 26

Isaiah 53:3 We despised him and rejected him - a man of sorrows, acquainted with bitterest grief. We turned our backs on him and looked the other way when he went by.

Jim Adams pondered this verse from Isaiah. "Here the Messiah was being described in Isaiah way before Jesus was born. Jesus indeed was a man of sorrows. Many did turn their backs on him. He was killed by those who rejected him. Have we learned anything from his great sacrifice? Not really. Each generation seems to turn their backs on him and look the other way as the Spirit of Jesus passes by. If he came into the world today, we would still reject him. Yet, through the love and grace of God, many in each generation do recognize, Jesus, the man of sorrows. Many do turn toward and follow him as his spirit passes by. His love is for every one of us in each generation. All we need to do is turn toward him and follow him."

**If Jesus came into the world today, do you think you would be able to recognize him?**

**Why? Why not?**

# March 27

John 7: 37–38 On the last day, the climax of the holidays, Jesus shouted to the crowds, "If anyone is thirsty, let him come to me and drink. For the scriptures declare that rivers of living water shall flow from the inmost being of anyone who believes in me."

In Sara's imagination, she could see herself in the crowd listening to Jesus speak. "He looks so tall and so loving. I go through the crowd to get closer to him. I wonder what Jesus means about people being thirsty. I guess Jesus means that if people want to know more about God, then we should come to Jesus. It's so hard to understand what scripture is trying to say. I get so confused. Religious education has been very interesting this year, and slowly, I am beginning to learn a few things about the Lord. I know that God loves us and wants us to have a friendship with him, even though we can't see him. But, in my imagination, I can see him. I can see him look at me with love and compassion in his eyes. Thank you, Jesus."

**Are you able to read scripture and place yourself with your imagination into a scene from scripture?**

**What is your favorite scene?**


# March 28

John 6:35–36 Jesus replied, "I am the Bread of Life. No one coming to me will ever be hungry again. Those believing in me will never thirst. But the trouble is, as I have told you before, you haven't believed even though you have seen me."

Amy wondered what Jesus meant by being the Bread of Life. "Does he mean that he is the foundation of life? If we do allow God to be our foundation, we will feel a sense of peace. A lot to think about is that many of the people who saw Jesus in person, who were with him in scripture, didn't believe he was the Messiah, let alone the foundation of a fulfilling life. A life fulfilled with what? I become so confused. Here I am in high school, preparing for what I will do in my career in the world. Yet how do I balance that with learning to have God as my foundation? I guess it really is all me. I don't separate my life in the world away from my Christian life. They are all one in the same, based on the foundation of Christian values of love of God and love of neighbor. Please help me, God. Amen"

**What is the foundation of your life based on?**

**Is Jesus the bread of your life?**

# March 29

Romans 8:24 We are saved by trusting, and trusting means looking forward to getting something we don't yet have—for a man who already has something doesn't need to hope and trust that he will get it.

Jake felt that St. Paul must have been writing to him as well as to the Romans. "I've been working hard to keep my grades up so I can get a scholarship to college, and I sure don't have that scholarship yet. So trusting means looking forward to getting something I don't yet have. I need to trust that God wants what is best for me, even if I don't get a scholarship. From where I sit, that would be a disaster. But on the other hand, there are other ways I can help pay for college. So, God, at this time, I trust I have faith that you will help me get into a college. You want what is best for me. I do trust that all will be well for me. I will stop worrying about my grades. I will do my 'best' and leave the rest up to you."

**Are you able to trust God?**

**Do you have faith? Why? Why not?**

# March 30

Psalm 84:5–6 Happy are those who are strong in the Lord, who want above all else to follow your steps. When they walk through the Valley of Weeping, it will become a place of springs where pools of blessing and refreshment collect after the rains!

Amanda Adams remembered the sorrow she felt when a dear loved one died. "I felt like my heart would break. Yet, in the middle of my aching heart was a sense of strength, even though the Lord felt very far away at that time. Even though he seemed distant, I could sense that he was indeed sharing my sorrow. He too was crying, creating 'a place of springs where pools of blessing and refreshments collect after the rains.' It took a long time for me to heal. In my pain of sorrow came a new awareness about life and death. After a long struggle with the sorrow, I came out on the other side a stronger and more compassionate person. I thank you, Lord, for that source of strength that came to me in the middle of that sorrow. Thank you for sharing the sorrow with me. Amen."

**Do you think that you are strong in the Lord?**

**What have been those times of the Valley of Weeping for you? Did they turn into pools of blessings and refreshment?**

# March 31

Psalm 103:13–16 He is like a father to us, tender and sympathetic to those who reverence him. For he knows we are but dust, and that our days are few and brief, like grass, like flowers, blown by the wind and gone forever.

"This verse gives me food for thought," Jim Adams quietly whispered. "I remember a time when I thought I would live this earthly life forever, but time and age have taught me that life on earth is indeed short. We humans are like grass and flowers, blown by the wind and gone forever. Our Lord promised us the good news of an eternal life when he rose from the dead and went to live forever with the Father. We humans are only dust in the world, but we can also live forever with God. I do think of God as a tender and sympathetic Father who guides us, confronts us, and is firm with us. He wants to have a relationship with us. He wants us to love him and to love each other. I know how much I love my children, so I can almost imagine how much God loves us. Thank you for your guidance, dear Father. Amen."

**Do you think of God as tender and sympathetic?**

**At what times in your life have, you felt his compassion.**

# 4 April

## April 1

Deuteronomy 30:20 Choose to love the Lord your God and to obey him and cling to him, for he is your life.

There were many things in scripture that Ted didn't quite understand. "My religion education teacher has really been great, and slowly I am beginning to understand a few things. My trouble is that I really am enjoying my friends and the after school activities. I don't think a lot about my schoolwork, I'm sorry to say, and I don't think often about God, either. Yet, I really do want to love God, and I feel that I really do love God. I want to do what I think he wants me to do, although many times I feel God wouldn't be very happy with me. I don't understand about clinging to him, though. I can't really say that God is my life, either. I would like to love, obey, cling to him, and for him to be my life, but right now I just have too many other things to do. I have a feeling that I need to pray for a deeper faith and trust that one step at a time, I will be able to feel that God is my life."

**Do you want God to be your life? Why? Why not?**

**As you grow older, are you growing closer to the Lord?**

# April 2

Joshua 24:25 So Joshua made a covenant with them that day at Shechem, committing them to a permanent and binding contract between themselves and God.

Sally was almost too young to actively take part in the family scripture prayer time; yet, the example her family set with listening to the verses from scripture and sitting silently in thought and prayer was making an impression on her. "I have a story book about a man named Joshua. Mommie read it to me the other day. The other man in the story was Moses. They were really nice men, and God liked them a lot. I visit God when we go to church, but Mommie says that God is everywhere. He is with me all the time as well as at church. God said he would be with Joshua and the people Joshua was taking care of! God, I love you. Thank you for loving me, too. Amen."

**Do you have the child like faith of Sally?**

**If you made a contract with God, what would it say?**

# April 3

Hebrews 2:18 For since he himself has now been through suffering and temptation, he knows what it is like when we suffer and are tempted and he is wonderfully able to help us.

This reading meant a lot to Amy. Not long ago, she learned in religion class that Jesus is often called the Wounded Healer. "Jesus, you really are the 'Wounded Healer.' You really do understand what it means to be human. You understand what it means to be a teenager, too. You take what is troubling us seriously. Nothing is too small for us to share with you. We can share our hopes, joys, and dreams with you, as well as our fears, anxieties, and tears. I ask you to help me to do what is right, yet I know you understand the struggle I have in trying to follow what I know you want me to do. All I know is that I need your help. I can't do anything well in this life without your help. My Wounded Healer, I love you so much."

**Do you picture Jesus as your Wounded Healer?**

**Are you easily able to share with Jesus your hopes, dreams, and joys, as well as your fears, anxieties, and tears?**

# April 4

Philemon 1:6 I always thank God when I am praying for you, dear Philemon, because I keep hearing of your love and trust in the Lord Jesus and in his people. And I pray that as you share your faith with others, it will grip their lives too as they see the wealth of good things in you that come from Christ Jesus.

Jim Adams wondered to himself, "If I were St. Paul writing this letter, who would I address it to? Who do I know who is like Philemon? Well, there is our pastor, of course. He is always there for everyone. He always has compassion and love in his heart in his dealings with all people. Then there are the Carsons. What a caring couple they are. They make everyone feel loved and welcomed. There is Carl at work, who is a very successful, honest person who cares about people first and business second. There isn't a dishonest bone in his body, which shows a person can be successful in his career without stepping over everyone in the process. There are many people who have a wealth of good things in them that come from Jesus Christ. Thank you, God, for surrounding me with these wonderful people."

**List the names of people you could write to as St. Paul wrote to Philemon.**

**What are the special qualities that you admire in these people?**

# April 5

Colossians 3:15 Let the peace of heart which comes from Christ be always present in your hearts and lives, for this is your responsibility and privilege as members of his body. And always be thankful.

Amy was again depressed this evening. "Why don't I feel the peace that is supposed to come from Christ and always be present in my heart? Is it because I worry too much? Have I gotten in a bad habit of negative thinking? I read somewhere that we are our thoughts. So if I am always a depressed, worrying type person, it is because my thoughts are negative and anxious. Yes, I believe this is so. Jesus, how can I drop this bad habit of looking on the downside of everything, including myself? I have low self-esteem. How did I get this way? Lord, please help me to think positive thoughts. I want to think well of myself just because I know you love me. Help me to turn over all my worries, fears, and negative thoughts to you each morning. Guide me. Heal my bad habit of negative thinking."

**Are your thoughts negative or positive?**

**Are you able to turn your life over to Jesus? Can you let go and let God?**

# April 6

Romans 12:15–16 When others are happy, be happy with them. If they are sad, share their sorrow. Work happily together. Don't try to act big. Don't try to get into the good graces of important people, but enjoy the company of ordinary folks. And don't think you know it all.

Tears welled up in Sara's eyes. "God, I am not at all happy that Jody won the spelling bee and I came in second. I find it much easier at times to share someone's hurts than to share their happiness. I guess I am jealous. I am comparing myself to Jody and others, and most of the time; I don't feel like I measure up. But then I feel that Jody really acted stuck up. Winning that spelling bee really went to her head. She acted like she was just too good to be around the ordinary kids like me. She acted like she had all of the answers to everything. She is a know-it-all! Oh, God, how would I have acted, though, if I had won the spelling bee? Would I have acted like a know-it-all too? Would I have ignored my ordinary friends? I must remember to always be myself and not let honors, rewards, or winning anything goes to my head."

**How do you behave when you win something?**

**How do you act when you lose?**

# April 7

Psalm 34: 18–19 The Lord is close to those whose hearts are breaking. He rescues those who are humbly sorry for their sins. The good man does not escape all troubles—he has them too. But the Lord helps him in each and every one.

These two verses touched Amanda Adams's heart deeply. She remembered the times in her life when her heart was breaking. "Yes, Lord, you were right by my side, even though most of the time I felt you were very far away. When a person's heart is broken, it is not possible to feel much more than the isolating pain of sorrow for a time. Then, God, my awareness of your loving presence would finally break through my sorrow and a bit of peace would flood my heart. I would then be so sorry that for a time I had turned away from you. But you were always there waiting for me to break through the pain and finally accept your healing love. None of us humans escapes the troubles this world has in store for us. But it is so comforting to know you are at our side, waiting for us to allow your comforting grace to enter our lives.

**When has the Lord been at your side to offer his healing love?**

**Did you accept his love and comfort?**

# April 8

Matthew 11: 18–19 "For John the Baptist doesn't even drink wine and often goes without food, and you say, 'He's crazy.' And I, the Messiah, feast and drink, and you complain that I am a glutton and a drinking man, and hang around with the worst of sinners! But brilliant men like you can justify your every inconsistency!"

"Oh, wow! How true!" Jim Adams sighed. "Every time I watch the news or read the paper, I see the inconsistency of world leaders, countries, and self-interest groups—the world in general. Things that are good can be twisted to sound bad. Things that are bad are twisted to sound good. We easily put labels on each other. What is saddest of all is when we put labels on small children such as 'he is stupid' or 'she is dumb.' When we put our very young preschool children into school programs that label them smart, average, or immature, we give them an unrealistic sense of themselves. Perhaps we adults don't realize that children carry around a label we put on them for the rest of their lives. The inner child in the adult will need much healing if he has been labeled in a negative way."

**What are some examples of inconsistent thinking that have happened to you?**

**Do you label people?**

# April 9

1 Corinthians 15:1 Now let me remind you, brothers, of what the Gospel really is, for it has not changed—it is the same good news I preached to you before.

"What does St. Paul mean when he preaches about the good news?" pondered Jake. "What is the good news? Well, it means that Jesus died for our sins, he was buried, and then he rose from the dead. Okay. So there is life after death, and if we follow the teachings of Christ, we will have eternal life in heaven. Okay. But what about now? I believe that Jesus can save us from the bad things we do here on earth—if we will just turn to him and ask for his help. I have a bad temper. I have prayed for his help in trying to understand where my temper is coming from. I know I can't get over my bad habits by my sheer willpower. I need God's help. Even more important is that the good news is about God's love for us. He sent his son into the world to help us, to save us from ourselves and others. Thank you, God, for your love."

**What does the good news mean to you?**

**Can you count on your sheer willpower in overcoming your own bad habits?**

# April 10

Romans 1:12 Then too, I need your help, for I want not only to share my faith with you but to be encouraged by yours. Each of us will be a blessing to the others.

"That is just about what Mr. Lewis told us in religion class last Sunday," thought Jake. "Some of the guys asked Mr. Lewis why they had to go to church. Couldn't they talk to God on their own without having to go to church? Who needed it, anyway? Mr. Lewis told them that we all needed a place to gather together to share our faith and to give each other support. I know what the guys were saying because at times I have felt the same way. Yet, I find that if I do stay away from church, I tend to forget about God. Then I find life is one big struggle, and I just don't feel very good about myself. Mom and Dad encourage me to attend church with them, and deep down, I'm glad they do. Yeah, each of us is a blessing to each other. Believe me; I need all the encouragement I can get."

**When have you felt you needed encouragement?**

**Are you able to share your faith with someone else?**

# April 11

Isaiah 25:4 But to the poor, O Lord, you are a refuge from the storm, a shadow from the heat.

A sudden storm came up when Sara was walking to the park. "I saw the black clouds and bolts of lighting. I heard the sound of thunder; I was in front of our church and ran up to the door, which fortunately was unlocked. I felt the cool, dry air as I sat down in the pew. I heard the thunder and realized that I was really scared. I don't like thunderstorms at all. It had been hot all day, and the cool air felt good. God, your home, the church, was a place of safety from the storm for me. Yeah, it was also a shadow from the heat. Many of the kids at school don't go to church. I wonder why they don't go. If they don't know about church, then they probably wouldn't think of coming into church to get out of the heat and away from a storm. You do look after me, God, and you do know about my fears. You will help me know how to deal with them. Amen"

**Do you have a place to come out of the heat and out of the rain?**

**Where do you find comfort when you are afraid?**

# April 12

Colossians 3:21 Fathers, don't scold your children so much that they become discouraged and quit trying.

"St. Paul was sure right about that," thought Jim Adams. "My own Dad was on our backs all the time when we were growing up. In fact, there is still very little I do that pleases him. Fortunately, I realize that he really doesn't know any better. He thinks that pointing out what he feels are errors on our part is his duty as a parent. That's the way he was raised. Well, that kind of thinking, I pray, will end with me. When I look at Jake, Amy, Sara, Ted, and little Sally, I see five children who are very vulnerable. They need all the love and encouragement that Amanda and I can give them. We want them to grow up to be loving, responsible, and self-confident adults. God, I pray that I will never put my kids down like my Dad does me. I pray that I will be able to give my children the loving kindness that you give us, God. I hope to give them unconditional love."

**Who in your life has given you encouragement?**

**In what ways was the encouragement given?**

# April 13

Rom 8:38 And I am convinced that nothing can ever separate us from his love. Death can't, and life can't. The angels can't, and the demons can't.

"I like to sing the song 'Jesus loves me, yes, I know,'" Sally giggled to herself. "Mommie tells me every night when I go to bed that she and Daddy and God love me so much. Even when I do something I shouldn't, like running into the street, I know that Mommie, Daddy, and God still love me. They don't want me in the street because I might be hit by a car. They don't want me to get hurt. When Mommie is mad at me, she tells me she still loves me but she just doesn't like what I did that made her mad. I guess God is the same way. He doesn't like what I do that is wrong, but he still loves me, anyway. Nothing will ever change his love for me. God, thank you for giving me my mommie and daddy and my sisters and brothers. Thank you for loving me, God."

**Do you think that God loves you no matter what you do?**

**Does he necessarily like what you do?**

# April 14

Psalm 116:1–2 I love the Lord because he hears my prayers and answers them because he bends down and listens, I will pray as long as I breathe!

Amanda Adams said, "I do love the Lord because he hears my prayers and he does indeed answer them. But more so, I love the Lord because he wants to have a relationship with each one of us. I love to pray because prayer is nothing more than holding a conversation with God, or sitting silently with the Lord and enjoying the quiet together. The Lord is my friend, and I am his friend. I ask him what he wants me to do each day. I tell him my cares and concerns just as I would to a close friend. But with the Lord, I can then hand over my cares and concerns knowing he will take good care of them. The Lord is always at my side, and I know I can do nothing without his help. Yes, God, I will pray as long as I breathe."

**How would you describe your prayer life?**

**Are you able to give over to the Lord your cares and your worries?**

# April 15

Colossians 4:2 Don't be weary in prayer; keep at it; watch for God's answers and remember to be thankful when they come.

Jim Adams felt like God didn't hear his prayers. "It is like talking to a concrete wall at times. I tell myself that listening to God during my prayer time, he will reveal his answer in his own way and own time. Sometimes I become weary while waiting for an answer. When I look back when things were deteriorating, I can now see how God was indeed listening and answering my prayers. The answer was not necessarily what I prayed for, but the outcome was brilliant. God always brought good out of each bad situation I encountered. Now when I begin to feel weary with my prayer, I remember and feel thankful for all of God's beautiful answers. Thank you, God. Amen."

**Have you ever felt weary in prayer?**

**Do you watch for God's answers?**


# April 16

1 Peter 2:25 Like sheep you wandered away from God, but now you have returned to your Shepherd, the Guardian of your souls who keeps you safe from all attacks.

Amy related to being like sheep. "I feel like one of a flock of sheep at school. I'm always trying to fit in, and it is a temptation for me to say yes to the many things these sheep want to do that I know isn't right. So when I say 'no,' I then am left out. But you know, God, you are my guardian, and you do keep me safe from all kinds of attacks we sheep are faced with. Drugs are becoming a real problem at school. A number of the kids at school get stoned just about everyday. They think it is cool, but I know it isn't cool at all. Drugs are ruining their lives. Then there is another group of kids who like to smoke, which can give them lung cancer, so I don't hang out with them either. I am considered to be a square at school. Thank you, God, for giving me the strength to be a square. I keep those kids in my prayers. I know you love them and want me to love them and pray for them.

**Do you feel that others think of you as a square?**

**Do you keep these people in your prayers?**

# April 17

2 Corinthians 1:3 What a wonderful God we have—he is the Father of our Lord Jesus Christ, the source of every mercy, and the one who so wonderfully comforts and strengthens us in our hardships and trials.

Jake sighed, "Yes, God, last week when I received that letter from the college I wanted to go to saying I hadn't been accepted, I felt like my world had collapsed. That was the only college I wanted to go to. I was mad at you, God, and I was mad at myself and everyone else, too. I felt sorry for myself and felt that my whole life would be a failure because of this rejection. When I finally talked to you about my anger, fear, and disappointment, I felt a peace come over me. I knew that you did understand my disappointment and that you would indeed give me the strength to overcome the rejection. A few days later, I heard from another college that they had accepted me. In fact, I learned that this college had a better program in the field I wanted to major in. So it's a good thing I wasn't accepted by the college of my choice. I thank you, God, for watching over me. Amen."

**Have you had disappointments and felt mad at God?**

**Did God give you the strength you needed to get through the disappointment?**

# April 18

Isaiah 53:1 But, oh, how few believe it! Who will listen? To whom will God reveal his saving power?

Amanda Adams wondered to herself, "Why do we humans ignore God's love? Is it because we can't see him? But then even when Jesus walked the earth, people ignored his message. So it isn't necessary to be able to see God. We still don't listen. Is it because we humans have the human condition? Is it a condition made up of pride; of greed; of possessions; of narrow selfish minds? Is it because we believe that each of us is in control of our own destiny? It is hard for us humans to have the humility of realizing that we are not in control of our lives, and that we are completely dependent on God to be saved from our own selfish desires and negative thinking. God gives us free will. It is our choice to choose between depending on God's helping grace or our own pitiful attempts of control. Unfortunately, too many of us choose to live life without God's help. I put these people in my prayers, handing them over to your tender loving care."

**Have you accepted God's helping grace in your life?**

**Are you able to listen to what God is telling you?**

# April 19

Isaiah 53:7 He was oppressed and he was afflicted, yet he never said a word. He was brought as a lamb to the slaughter; and as a sheep before her shearers is dumb so he stood silent before the one's condemning him.

Amy often thought about Jesus, the Son of God, not being accepted in the world. "I don't like to have anyone misunderstand me and jump to wrong conclusions about me. Somehow, when this happens to me, I always think of Jesus and I feel comforted. I know that he understands so well, how hurt I feel, and he is standing by, waiting for me to give him my hurt feelings to heal. I hear him telling me that instead of nursing anger toward these people, I put them into his loving care right along with my hurting feelings. I know I must stop allowing people power over how I think about myself. With the Lord's help, I will be able to get my self worth from deep inside me instead of from things and people outside myself."

**Where does your sense of well being come from?**

**Do you allow outside things and people affect your sense of self worth?**

# April 20

Isaiah 53:10–11 He shall live again and God's program shall prosper in his hands. And when he sees all that is accomplished by the anguish of his soul, he shall be satisfied.

Jim Adams at one time tried to figure out everything he read in scripture. "I wanted to know the whys, what ifs, and make everything logical. Why did God send his son to save us? Because he loves us. How can it be that Jesus was able to come back to life? To show us there is eternal life; victory over death. Why did Jesus have to suffer? The most important thing in the life of humankind was accomplished by the anguish of the soul of Jesus. He opened the door between our Father and us humans. But why? Why does God want us to have a relationship with him? Why does he even care? It's a mystery; a beautiful, life-giving mystery and I accept the mystery. I have stopped questioning. I realize my mind doesn't think like God. My ways are not God's ways. Isn't that wonderful? Thank you, God, for the grace of faith."

**Have you accepted God's mysteries?**

**Do you accept that God's ways are not our ways?**

# April 21

Psalm 118:8–9 It is better to trust the Lord than to put confidence in men. It is better to take refuge in him than in the mightiest king.

Ted remembered the day when he had really been let down by his best friend, Phil. "Yeah, I was counting on Phil to work with me on a science project at school. Well, he backed out at the last minute, saying he wasn't going to get involved with the Science Fair this year. So here I was, stuck doing this project alone. I sure can't count on anyone's help. Well, as it all turned out, I became engrossed with the project, and was glad I was working on it alone. I know that God was helping me because I turned to him for guidance. What I later learned was that Phil's family was having a crisis and he wasn't able to find the extra time or energy for a science project. He didn't want to share his problems with me, nor did I encourage him to share. So I let him down too. When he needed understanding, I gave him a sharp tongue and a cold shoulder. I am sorry, and I must apologize to Phil."

**Have you let anyone down who needed you? Have you been let down?**

**Who should you turn to each moment?**

# April 22

John 12:9–11 When the ordinary people of Jerusalem heard of his arrival, they flocked to see him and also to see Lazarus—the man who had come back to life again. Then the chief priests decided to kill Lazarus too, for it was because of him that many of the Jewish leaders had deserted and believed in Jesus as their Messiah.

Shaking his head, Jim Adams sighed, "Aren't we humans something else? Here are intelligent Jewish leaders who are caught up in their narrow, rigid thinking. They think that the solution to their problems with Jesus was to kill him. They wanted to kill Lazarus also because Jesus had raised him from the dead. How could they solve the problem of stopping people from deserting them? People were following Jesus because he raised Lazarus from the dead. What is frightening to me, though, is the fact that if I was one of the Jewish leaders, would I too have this twisted thinking? I firmly believe in the saying 'There but for the grace of God go I.' We humans can come up with some pretty twisted ideas. God save me from myself. Amen"

**What are your thoughts about the Jewish leaders?**

**Do you see any of their rigid traits in yourself?**

# April 23

Ezekiel 37:12–13 But tell them, the Lord God says: "My people, I will open your graves of exile and cause you to rise again and return to the land of Israel. And, then at last, O my people, you will know that I am the Lord."

With a heavy heart, Amy thought of Bev, who was in her homeroom. "Bev has had so many problems, and I wonder where she is. I couldn't believe it when I heard that she had run away from home. I pray that she is okay. Only a year ago, Bev had everything going for her. Then some problems developed in her family, and she became withdrawn and dropped out of all her school activities. She stopped going to church, also. It is like Bev is in a grave of exile. God, I ask you to open Bev's grave of exile and heal her wounds. Bring her back to us and to church. Tell us what we, as her friends, can do to help her heal. I know that you have such a great love for Bev and for all of us. You want only good things to happen to Bev. I pray that she will turn to you for help. Amen"

**Have you ever been in what felt like a grave of exile?**

**What brought you back home?**

# April 24

John 13:34 "And so I am giving a new commandment to you now—love each other just as much as I love you. Your strong love for each other will prove to the world that you are my disciples."

Sara was really getting angry at a few kids at school who were picking on her and teasing her. "I don't know what I ever did to them to make them want to tease me like they do. They are bullies, and they pick on other kids, too. There are days I hate them because they are so mean. I wish someone would punish them. So here, Jesus is saying to love one another as he loves us. Would Jesus love those bullies? Yes, I guess he would. I know he doesn't like what they are doing, but he does love them, and he is asking me to love them, too. How can I love them? What kind of love? Maybe love means to wish them the best. It means to try to understand and pray for them. I will put them in God's care. I must not hate them, nor wish for bad things to happen to them. That will hurt me, and I won't be a disciple of Christ. Help me, God, to love them. Amen."

**Has a bully ever picked on you?**

**What was your reaction?**

# April 25

Mark 14:24–25 And he said to them, "This is my blood, poured out for many, sealing the new agreement between God and man. I solemnly declare that I shall never again taste wine until the day I drink a different kind in the Kingdom of God."

Amanda Adams thought about the scene of the Last Supper. "I can imagine how bewildered the disciples were, sitting there listening to Jesus. I am also bewildered by the mystery of it all. But out of it all, a new agreement was sealed between God and man through the sacrifice of Jesus and the resurrection. We humans think we are so smart, so intelligent. But all reasoning intellect will do us not one bit of good in trying to figure any of this mystery out. We must come to the Last Supper as the disciples did. They couldn't understand God's plan. They did not know what Jesus was about, but they knew they loved Jesus deep within their hearts. I too want to love Jesus deep within my heart and accept the mysteries with the faith of a child."

**Can you imagine yourself joining the disciples in the scene of the Last Supper?**

**What is your reaction?**

# April 26

John 18:36 Then Jesus answered, "I am not an earth King. If I were, my followers would have fought when I was arrested by the Jewish leaders. But my kingdom is not of the world."

Ted Adams nodded his head. "No, Jesus, your kingdom is not of the world. The world is filled with many good people who are trying to do what is right; people who have values. But there are those in the world who are filled with greed, jealousy, malice, gluttony, and vain pride. They have no love for anyone, and if it were investigated, they really have no love for themselves, either. Yet, you love and care about those people as well as those who are trying to do what is right. The key here is that God has given us freedom of choice. We can choose to learn about him and his ways, which are to love God, love each other, and to love ourselves. Jesus is the King of God's kingdom. The kingdom of the world is full of hate, competition, war, and all of the negative things that an earthly king has rule over. Jesus rules the kingdom of God's love."

**Can you describe what the kingdom of the world means to you?**

**Where do you find the kingdom of God?**


# April 27

John 21:12–14 "Now come and have some breakfast!" Jesus said; and none of us dared ask him if he really was the Lord for we were quite sure of it. Then Jesus went around showing us the bread and fish. This was the third time, Jesus had appeared to us since he returned from the dead.

Jake pictured himself sitting on the beach with the disciples as Jesus served them the bread and fish. "The wonder of it all. To think this man who we loved so much was serving the bread and the fish. The man who we thought was dead was here on this beach with us. This was the third time we had seen him since he returned from the dead. What did Jesus want of us? What did Jesus want his disciples to do? He told Peter to take care of his sheep, to feed them. The disciples were supposed to tell the story about Jesus, his death, and his resurrection to everyone they met. And I, too, twenty-one centuries in the future, am supposed to spread the good news of the Lord. The good news is that God loves us and he wants a relationship with us. All we have to do is to turn toward him and ask for his help in guiding us toward him."

**Can you picture yourself sitting on the beach with the resurrected Lord and the disciples?**

**What does Jesus ask of you?**

# April 28

Acts 10:42–43 And he ordered us to preach everywhere and to testify that Jesus is ordained of God to be the judge of all—the living and the dead. He is the one all the prophets testified about, saying that everyone who believes in him will have their sins forgiven through his name."

Amy pondered the line saying that everyone who believes in him will have their sins forgiven through his name. "I don't quite understand about having sins forgiven through his name. One way I can look at it is that when we meet Jesus, just knowing him makes us aware of our bad habits. When we turn our eyes and our hearts toward Jesus, we slowly but surely will try to be loving and compassionate like him. We need to ask for his help, though. There is a mystery here that I can't begin to understand. That's okay, though. Jesus, please help me in trying to do what you would like me to do. Amen."

**How much do you know about Jesus?**

**What would you be able to tell others about Jesus?**

# April 29

Acts 11:19–21 Meanwhile, the believers who fled from Jerusalem during the persecution after Stephen's death traveled as far as Phonenicea, Cyprus, and Antioch, scattering the good news, but only to the Jews.

Jake remembered his religion teacher saying that some of the believers also gave the message about Jesus to the Greeks, also. "It is awesome to think about how fast the news about Jesus traveled. They didn't have radio, telephones, or television in those days. Mass communications were unheard of. Despite that fact, the good news spread mostly by word of mouth. The news about Jesus is just as fresh and alive today as it was back in those days. There are of course people who refuse to listen and to believe, as was the case back then. The human condition lives on. I know a lot of the guys at school don't think going to church is a very cool thing. I put them in my prayers, and pray that one day they will be open to hearing what the Lord has to say."

**Do you know very many people who absolutely refuse to listen to what God is saying?**

**What is your prayer for them?**

# April 30

John 10:2–4 "For a Shepherd comes through the gate. The gatekeeper opens the gate for him and the sheep hear his voice and come to him; and he calls his own sheep by name and leads them out. He walks ahead of them; and they follow him, for they recognize his voice."

Sally remembered a picture in her Bible Story Book showing Jesus holding a lamb. She once visited a farm where she saw some sheep in the pasture, so she tried to imagine herself standing in the pasture with the sheep. "Here comes Jesus through the gate. He is speaking softly to the sheep. They hear him and walk over to him. I follow the sheep, and I feel safe. I know Jesus loves me. He turns towards the gate, and the sheep follow him through the gate and out of the pasture. Should I follow him also? I'm not sure, but now I see Mommie and Daddy reach out their hands to me, and we follow Jesus and the sheep through the gate. I still need my mommie and daddy with me. When I get big, then maybe I can walk out the gate alone. I need to get to know Jesus better I guess."

**Are you able to walk out the gate alone? Or do you need to get to know Jesus better before you can?**

**Can you recognize the voice of our Lord calling you?**

# 5 May

## May 1

2 Corinthians 4:8–9 We are pressed on every side by troubles, but not crushed and broken. We are perplexed because we don't know why things happen as they do, but we don't give up and quit. We are hunted down but God never abandons us.

Amanda Adams remembered the illness and death of her good friend, Charlotte. "Everything seemed to be going wrong in my life at that time, but I did have the wisdom and understanding of Charlotte. Then suddenly Charlotte died, leaving me feeling abandoned and alone in a town far away from my family and friends. Charlotte and her family had a strong faith in Jesus Christ. It was through Charlotte's death that I came back to God and to the teachings of my childhood. That was the beginning of my maturity and the end of my rebellion. No wonder I felt I had problems all around me. I hadn't been allowing the Lord to guide me. I didn't give up and quit. I knew that Charlotte wanted me to live a full and happy life. The only way I could do that was to allow the Lord into my life to guide me as he had guided Charlotte. In due time, I met Jim, and both of us turned to you with love. Thank you, Lord."

**Have you ever felt alone and abandoned?**

**When did you first realize how important the Lord is in your life?**

# May 2

2 Corinthians 4:6 For God, who said, "Let there be light in the darkness," has made us understand that it is the brightness of his glory that is seen in the face of Jesus Christ.

Amy's religion education teacher made it a big point to stress that Jesus is the light of the world. Amy pondered, "Before Christ came to the earth, the people seemed to have a hard time in keeping in touch with God. Then he sent his son, Jesus, to be a bridge between God and his people. His son was a human, just like us, except he never sinned. But nonetheless, he had feelings just like us. He had compassion and showed us God's mercy and love for us. Even though we have the good news about Jesus, people still have a hard time keeping in touch with God. But Jesus is and has been the light in the darkness of each person's soul. If only we could turn our eyes toward the light shining in our souls. There, we could find the peace and the joy God wants for each of his children."

**Have you been following the light shining in the darkness of your soul?**

**Do you believe that Jesus is the light of the world?**

# May 3

1 John 3:18–19 Little children, let us stop just saying we love people; let us really love them and show it by our actions. Then we will know for sure, by our actions that we are on God's side, and our consciences will be clear, even when we stand before the Lord.

Sara wondered if she could stand before the Lord with a clear conscience. "Just the other day, I gossiped about one of the girls at school. I know why I was trying to tear her down in the eyes of others. I was jealous of her, and I tore her down to build myself up. I say I love and care about everyone, and yet every once in a while, I will run into a situation where I will tear someone down to make myself look better. That certainly isn't a loving thing to do. When I tear people down, I am not on your side, am I, God? I'm so sorry. I need your help in showing me how to love people. Help me to understand people and to forgive people. Show me how to pray for others. I love you, God. Help me to love others too. Amen."

**Can you stand before the Lord with a clear conscience?**

**Do your actions show that you are on God's side?**

# May 4

John 15:5 "Whoever lives in me and I in him shall produce a large crop of fruit. For apart from me, you can't do a thing."

Sara wondered what kind of fruit Jesus was talking about. "What does he mean? Oh, I remember hearing about a term called fruits of the spirit. If I really do care about the kids at school, then my caring will show in my actions. If someone is sad and I try to comfort that person, then the fruit of that action on my part will be that person will know someone cares about her and will feel better. Jesus is saying that we need his help to bring about a large crop of fruit. We can't bring about good fruit without his help. Well, that is true. I'm just a kid, and I know I need the help of Mom and Dad, and I need the help of the Lord to help me be a good person."

**What kind of fruit do you produce?**

**Do you need the Lord's help in all things?**

# May 5

Psalm 16:3–4 I want the company of the godly men and women in the land; they are the true nobility. Those choosing other gods shall all be filled with sorrow.

Amy thought back on a party she attended several weeks ago. "I was happy that Cass invited me to her party. Cass is in with the party group at school, and I really wanted to be popular. What a horrible experience it turned out to be. When Mom asked me who was going to be at the party and if the parents were going to be there, I assured her everything would be okay. She told me she would pick me up at 11:00 that evening, and I really made a fuss about it. I told her she was treating me like a baby. I felt very excited when I arrived at the party. Then I noticed that there were kids there I didn't know. Cass and her friends were smoking funny looking cigarettes. Some of the guys were drinking, too. They got loud. Then I found out that the parents weren't at home. When the kids wanted me to take a drink, I said no! At 11:00, Mom arrived, and I got into the car and cried. Oh, God, I thank you for guiding me away from bad friendships. Thank you for the Godly friendships I have."

**Who are the Godly people you know?**

**Why do those who choose other Gods fill up with sorrow?**

# May 6

Acts 13:45 But when the Jewish leaders saw the crowds, they were jealous, and cursed and argued against whatever Paul said.

Jake remembered the class elections at the beginning of the school year. "I acted like a fool when I lost the election for class president to Al. I sincerely thought Al was a jerk, and I couldn't understand how any of the class could vote for him. I found myself voting down any suggestion Al would make as president of our class. I wanted to prove to everyone that Al didn't know what he was doing. I wanted them to know that they made a mistake in voting for Al instead of me. Al was doing a good job, and everyone thought he was great. I was acting like those Jewish leaders. I hate to admit it, but when I saw how everyone liked Al, I became jealous and furious. How could I have done that? Al and I have become friends. When I let go of my disappointment of losing the election, I could finally see Al's good qualities. Thank you, God, for helping me work through my jealousy."

**Have you ever been jealous?**

**What were the results of that jealousy?**

# May 7

Acts 18:9 One night the Lord spoke to Paul in a vision and told him, "Don't be afraid! Speak out! Don't quit! For I am with you and no one can harm you."

Amanda Adams belonged to a woman's group that she really enjoyed until just recently. A subtle change had begun to take place. "I can't put my finger on where this gossiping started. It was so innocent in the beginning, but lately the gossip has become very damaging. I have been coming home feeling depressed, and I've been thinking about quitting. Yes, Lord, I can hear you say deep in my heart for me to speak out about the gossiping. I need to mention the damage it is doing to everyone, including the ones doing the gossiping. I know you don't want me to quit, either. That wouldn't help me, and it wouldn't help anyone else, either. Oh, but Lord, I am so afraid to speak up. I know, Lord. You are with me. You will guide me in gently telling these women about the trap of gossiping we have fallen into. The time has come to bring the group back to the positive objectives we once had."

**Have you ever been tempted to quit when a situation got tough?**

**What made you hang in there?**

# May 8

Romans 8:25 But we must keep trusting God for something that hasn't happened yet. It teaches us to wait patiently and confidently.

Ted sighed to himself thinking, "I'm sick of being told to be patient. All I hear is 'Be patient, Ted, be patient.' I can't stand waiting for the unknown. I want the answers now so I can move on to something new. When I take a test, I want to know the results right then and there. Our dog, Ginger, is sick. I wonder what is wrong with her. This afternoon when I came home from school, I found Ginger lying on her bed. She didn't move when I called for her to come over to see me. Mom and I took her to the vet, where they are keeping her over night. They gave her an IV so she would have fluids since she wouldn't eat or drink any water. Oh, God, I've got to trust that she is okay. If Ginger isn't okay, I will have to trust you to give me the strength and the courage to get through the hurt of losing her. Oh, God, I am so afraid." Suddenly a feeling of peace came over Ted. He knew deep in his heart that Ginger was going to be okay.

**Do you have patience?**

**Are you able to trust God in all things? If not, name the things that worry you.**

# May 9

Galatians 2:20 I myself no longer live, but Christ lives in me.

"Boy, that is a powerful verse," thought Jim Adams. "There was a time when I felt I knew all the answers to a full and happy life. I thought that having a powerful job, a big house, a big car, and lots of money left over would give happiness. I wanted to be involved in the community not for the betterment of the community, but instead for the betterment of my ego. I wanted to control, to be well known, to have status. Wow, was I surprised when I found myself burned out. I decided to go back to church, and there I found Christ. I studied the gospels and discovered that the emptiness I had been feeling was being filled up. Jesus' commandments were to love God with all your heart and soul, and to love your neighbor as yourself. Well, I started to love myself, and then I was able to love my neighbor. I was filled with deep love for God. Thank you for being with me and in me, Christ."

**What do you think a person needs for a happy life?**

**What does the word "happy" mean to you?**


# May 10

Leviticus 26:1–2 "You must have no idols; you must never worship carved images, obelisks, or shaped stones, for I am the Lord your God."

"God wants us to worship only him," Amy thought to herself. "What does it mean to worship images, obelisks, or shaped stones? I don't understand. I wonder what could be thought of as idols in this day and age. What are our idols today that we worship? What do we get caught up in that would keep us from thinking of God? Well, I guess that could be the addictions to drugs and alcohol. A person can be a workaholic or have an obsession with money. The occult is a god. We need to lean completely on God. Only he is able to give us that deep down peace we are looking for. Idols will let us down every time."

**What are your idols?**

**How can you overcome worshipping these idols?**

# May 11

1 Peter 2:1 So get rid of your feelings of hatred. Don't pretend to be good. Be done with dishonesty and jealousy and talking about others behind their backs.

"Oh no, here we go again," Sara sighed to herself. "I've been thinking I have been such a great person since I won first place in the art contest. I was so happy that I beat out that Hillary, who I really began to hate because she was always getting compliments on her artwork. Oh no, I couldn't help myself. I actually gloated about winning over Hillary. I talked about her behind her back. I even went so far as to say she traced some of her art that was often hanging on the bulletin board. Why have I been so jealous of Hillary? She is really a very nice girl, and she would never hurt me. Why do I want to hurt her? Oh God, please help me be nice to Hillary, and to want her to have the best of everything. Please help me work through this jealous streak I have in me. Help me to feel good about myself. Thank you."

**Have you ever had a jealous streak in you?**

**What happened?**

# May 12

Psalm 31:1 Lord, I trust in you alone. Don't let my enemies defeat me. Rescue me because you are the God who always does what is right.

Jake paused with the thought, "Enemies—I don't have any enemies. What kind of enemies in my life could defeat me? Yet, I feel this verse applies to something way deep inside of me. Enemies. I guess enemies could be addictions to drugs. I have sure seen some of the kids at school become addicted, and what an enemy they have to fight. There are times when the drugs do defeat them. I guess they didn't know that God would help them if only they would ask him to. I suppose that we can be our own worst enemy when we become hard on ourselves, when we drive ourselves for a perfection that just isn't there. Not expecting enough out of ourselves and not living up to our potential isn't good for us, either. God, I pray that you won't let my faults defeat me. I trust you to help me, God. Amen."

**What are your enemies?**

**Do you trust God to help you deal with your enemies?**

# May 13

Jeremiah 23:23 Am I a God who is only in one place and cannot see what they are doing? Can anyone hide from me? Am I not everywhere in all of heaven and earth?

Sally thought about God saying he is everywhere. "I wonder how God can be everywhere all at the same time? God knows everything we are doing. Did you see me run into the street this morning, God? I guess you did, because Mom came right after me and told me I could spend some time in my room to think about what not going into the street. You and Mom want to protect me, don't you,

God? You don't want me to get hurt. At first, I felt afraid, thinking you were watching everything I do. But it is nice of you to care about me. I'm glad you are with me, God. Thank you."

**How do you feel about not being able to hide from God?**

**Have you ever tried to hide from God?**

# May 14

1 Peter 5:7 Let him have all your worries and cares, for he is always thinking about you and watching everything that concerns you.

"Oh, God, if I only would realize deep in my heart that I should let you have all my worries and cares," sighed Amy. "I know this in my head, but in my heart I am full of anxiety and worry and fear. People call me a worrywart. I can't have fun because I am always worried about something in the past, the present, and the future. This being over-responsible started out in elementary school. It is now nothing but a bad habit, and a habit that is taking joy away from my life. It is a good trait to be a responsible person, but when it is carried to an extreme, such as in my case, it is a bad habit. God, I pray to you to guide me in learning when to take care of things that I can take care of. I need to let you have the things I can't do anything about, and the knowledge to know the difference."

**Are you able to let God have your worries?**

**Are you able to trust God that he will take good care of things, allowing him to do so in his way and in his time?**

# May 15

Ezekiel 34:15 I myself will be the Shepherd of my sheep, and cause them to lie down in peace, the Lord God says. I will seek my lost ones, those who strayed away, and bring them safely home again. I will put splints and bandages upon their broken limbs and heal the sick.

"What a beautiful verse," Jim Adams thought to himself. "I was one of those sheep who strayed away thinking I didn't need God. I felt that I alone was in control of my destiny and my life. For a while, everything went according to my plans for my life. I had a good education, a good job—a good everything. Then I lost my job and was over qualified for other jobs, so I was out of work for a long time. I remember the evening when I felt a great despair of emptiness and loneliness. I was furious with God for allowing this to happen to me. Then it came to me that I had turned away from God and that I needed to ask for his courage and strength. When things were going well, I took credit. When things went bad, I blamed God. You put splints and bandages on my broken spirit, and I was healed."

**Have there been times in your life when you took credit for things that went well and blamed God for the things that went wrong?**

**When has God put splints and bandages on your broken spirit?**

# May 16

Isaiah 41:10 Fear not, for I am with you. Do not be dismayed. I am your God. I will strengthen you; I will help you; I will uphold you with my victorious right hand.

Amanda Adams's eyes filled with tears as she listened to Jake read this verse. "Oh, God, I needed to hear these words telling me not to be afraid and dismayed. You are with me and you will give me strength. Why is it that I need to be reminded each and every day that no matter what, you will give me strength? For that reason, I need not be afraid or depressed. Oh, if only I had the trust that you will give me strength deep in my heart. I am continually fighting anxiety and fears, which come from my doubting heart. God, I am too weak to heal my doubting heart by sheer will power. In my weakness, I am forced to rely on your help. In my weakness comes your strength. Help me realize deep within my heart that you are upholding me with your victorious right hand."

**Do you ever feel dismayed? What helps you?**

**Do you feel that God is indeed with you?**

# May 17

1 Timothy 1:15–16 How true it is, and how I long that everyone should know it, that Christ Jesus came into the world to save sinners. And I was the greatest of them all. But God had mercy on me so that Christ Jesus could use me as an example to show everyone how patient he is with even the worse sinners, so that others will realize that, they too can have everlasting life.

Jake couldn't imagine that St. Paul would have really done anything wrong. Then Jake remembered that St. Paul was Saul, who persecuted Christians before Christ came into his life. "God does show mercy through Jesus Christ. Mom says that I seem to put myself into the position of learning things the hard way. I guess St. Paul had to learn things the hard way, also. Maybe all of us have to learn many things the hard way. Jesus is there to help us, to forgive us, to show mercy to us if only we will turn to him and ask for his help. How many times do I do what I think is okay, only to later realize that it wasn't okay? Jesus, be with me to show me the right path. Amen."

**When have you felt God's mercy?**

**Do you have to learn things the hard way? Where is God in this learning process for you?**

# May 18

Colossians 3:12–13 Because of his deep love and concern for you, you should practice tenderhearted mercy and kindness to others. Be gentle and ready to forgive; never hold grudges.

Amy prayed, "God, please help me be kind to others. I know you love me, but I find it so hard to think that many people don't have a deep concern about me, and that hurts. I want people to like me and to care about what happens to me. Instead, it seems like many of them are truly happy when bad things happen to me. They want to put me down. I guess it makes them feel superior. So what do I feel like doing to them? I hold a grudge against them. I don't want to forgive them. I know that all of this grudge-holding business makes me mad, depressed, and unhappy. The only way I can feel peace is to let go of the grudge by forgiving them. Help me show them tenderhearted mercy and kindness. Help me to be gentle and to be ready to forgive."

**Have you ever held a grudge?**

**What did holding a grudge do to your peace of mind?**

# May 19

2 Corinthians 4:8–9 We are pressed on every side by troubles, but not crushed and broken. We are perplexed because we don't know why things happen as they do, but we don't give up and quit. We are hunted down, but God never abandons us.

Mrs. Lewis, Sara's religion teacher, had talked about this verse a few weeks before. "Mrs. Lewis explained that life was hard for St. Paul and his followers in the early church. I thought that since St. Paul was a Saint that everything went well for him. Mrs. Lewis said that they did indeed have lots of problems, but the important thing was that they weren't crushed and broken. They didn't give up and quit. Although they were hunted down, God never abandoned them. That's a good lesson for me to remember. No matter how badly things seem to be going for me, God is always the strength and courage I need for each task I do. I need only to turn to him and ask for his help."

**Have you ever felt crushed and broken by troubles?**

**Did you turn to God and ask him for his help?**


# May 20

Peter 2:1–3 So get rid of your feelings of hatred. Don't just pretend to be good! Be done with dishonesty and jealousy and talking about others behind their backs. Now that you realize how kind the Lord has been to you, put away all evil, deception, envy and fraud.

This verse hit home with Amy. "Oh, my Lord, I have been so jealous of everyone lately—almost to the point of hatred. Why am I so jealous? Why do I keep comparing myself to everyone else? Why do I constantly measure the attention everyone gets against the lack of attention I feel I receive? Who am I beginning to hate the most? It is me. If I really cared about myself, I wouldn't treat me as badly as I do when I say Julie is prettier than me, Jody gets better grades than me, Lora is liked by everyone and I'm not. I am being mean to myself. Then I lash out at others by talking about them behind their backs. I guess I am just pretending to be good. Help me to care about myself and not cut myself down. You have been kind to me, Lord. Help me love you, my neighbor, and myself. Amen."

**Have you ever been jealous?**

**Have you ever talked about others behind their backs? Why?**

# May 21

Galatians 5:14–15 For the whole Law can be summed up in one command: "Love others as you love yourself." But instead of showing love among yourselves, you are always critical and catty, watch out! Beware of ruining each other.

"I wish the people who serve on the board with me could read this verse," Amanda Adams reflected. "The board meeting I attended today was awful. We will never get this issue we have been working on for months settled if this critical, backbiting behavior continues. I feel torn to pieces by it. We are literally ruining each other, as well as the board we serve on. I am finding it very hard to love these people. It is so easy to love you, God, but it sometimes is nearly impossible to love people. I pray for your gift of insight and compassion for others. Help me to become an instrument of your peace so we can resolve with your help the issue that is tearing us apart. Help me with the anger I am feeling. Help me use the anger in a constructive way, in a positive way. With your grace, I have confidence that everything will be resolved in a positive way."

**Have you ever worked with critical, catty people?**

**How did you cope with them? Were you able to love them despite the fact that you didn't like what they were doing?**

# May 22

Romans 5:3–4 We can rejoice, too, when we run into problems and trials for we know that they are good for us—they help us learn to be patient. And patience develops strength of character in us and helps us trust God more each time we use it until finally our hope and faith are strong and steady.

"I don't like problems and trials," Amanda Adams said to herself. "Yet, I know that it is when things aren't going well that I am learning the most. As I grow older, I find that I grow in patience and love God more and more. I wish I could help my children understand that problems and trials are a necessary part of life. Our secular society gives all kinds of suggestions to escape problems. Instead, we need to be encouraged to learn how to be patient. Then we do indeed develop strength of character. When we lean on the Lord, and when we allow ourselves to rest in his love despite all the unrest going on around us—only then will our hope and faith become strong and steady. Thank you God for being with us in our struggles."

**How do you handle the problems that come your way?**

**Do you feel that problems and trials are good for you because they teach you patience?**

# May 23

Ephesians 5:1–2 Follow God's example in everything you do just as a much-loved child imitates his father.

Jake considered this verse. "I never thought about God as a father before. The other day, George, one of the guys at school, was really mad at his dad. He said his dad was always being critical and took out his frustrations on him. George wondered if his dad even loved him at all. Gosh, I really am lucky. My dad is the best, and I really do want to imitate my dad. The key here is that deep down, I know that Dad loves me. Even where we have disagreements, I know that Dad wants what is best for me. It is nice to realize that God loves me, too, and that God wants what is best for me also. With that in mind, I can follow God's example just as I follow Dad's example. I pray that George and his dad will make peace with each other, and that your love will heal their relationship. Amen"

**How do you view God?**

**Do you feel like a much-loved child of God?**

# May 24

Hebrews 13:1–2 Continue to love each other with true brotherly love. Don't forget to be kind to strangers, for some who have done this have entertained angels without realizing it!

This got Sally's interest. "Angels? I have a book that shows angels hovering over the stable where Jesus was born. Mommie said angels come from heaven. How can we entertain angels without us realizing it? I wonder if I have ever met an angel. Maybe I have and I didn't even know the person was an angel. Would they have wings? Maybe they hide their wings. I wonder what an angel would act like. Angels are kind and loving. Do I know anyone like that? Yes, there is Mommie and Daddy. They don't have wings, but they are nice and kind, and they love everyone. Could I ever be an angel? I bet I could be if I am nice and kind, and if I love everyone. God, help me to act like and angel. Amen."

**Have you ever entertained an angel without realizing it?**

**Do you believe in angels, and if so, what is an angel to you?**

# May 25

Psalm 31:7 I am radiant with joy because of your mercy, for you have listened to my troubles and have seen the crisis in my soul.

"What a beautiful thought," Amy reflected. "You know, God, I do feel radiant with joy. You have listened to my troubles, and you have seen the crisis in my soul. I am getting to the place where I don't feel as jealous of others like I once did. You are guiding me in showing me how to take good care of myself, and in turn, helping me to care about others as I care about myself. Yes, God, I am beginning to feel good about myself. I am not nearly as anxious as I used to be. I am feeling much more relaxed. Because I am becoming more relaxed with who I am, it seems like I am making more friends. People seem to want to be around me. Maybe it is because I no longer push people away. I feel they will like me because I now like myself. Oh, God, thank you for helping me. Amen."

**Has God listened to your troubles? Does he know the crisis in your soul?**

**How has God helped you?**

# May 26

1 Corinthians 13:13 There are three things that remain—faith, hope, and love—and the greatest of these is love.

Amanda Adams loved that verse. "Love is the greatest of faith, hope, and love. We need faith, and we certainly need hope, but all of us need to give and receive love. We hunger, we yearn for love. Without love, our works are nothing. Probably the hardest thing we have to do is to love a person we find very difficult to deal with. I remember Mrs. Lat, who I was terrified of when as a child. She was a neighbor of ours, and she was very hateful toward us. She was indeed hard to love. One day I asked my mother if I could take a dozen of the cookies we had baked over to give to Mrs. Lat. Mother looked at me and smiled. I took the cookies over and gave them to Mrs. Lat. She looked at the cookies, then at me, and tears filled her eyes. She invited me in, gave me a glass of milk, and we shared the cookies. After that, Mrs. Lat and I became very good friends. Yes, the greatest gift of all is love."

**Do you agree that the greatest gift of all is love?**

**Has there ever been a Mrs. Lat in your life?**


# May 27

Psalm 145:17–19 The Lord is fair in everything he does, and full of kindness. he is close to all who call on him sincerely. he fulfills the desires of those who reverence and trust him; he hears their cries for help and rescues them.

Jake thought about the coach at school. "Mr. Hay really isn't a very fair man. I'm glad that the baseball season is just about over and graduation is just around the corner. Just a couple more weeks, and I'm out of here. Mr. Hay sure has his favorites, and I'm not one of them. What if the Lord was our baseball coach? Wonder what he would do? Well, he would definitely be fair. He would give each of us a chance to play ball, not caring if we won the game or not. He wouldn't feel that winning was everything. The Lord would be kind, also. Mr. Hay isn't kind, that's for sure. Mr. Hay probably thinks I am a wimp, but I know that God thinks I'm a great person and loves me as I am. I'm sure glad that Mr. Hay isn't God. I would be in deep trouble. Thank you, God, for being you. Amen."

**Has there ever been a person like Mr. Hay in your life?**

**Do you turn to the Lord to ask him for his help?**


# May 28

Isaiah 63:8–9 He said, "They are my very own; surely they will not be false again." And he became their Savior. In all their affliction he was afflicted and he personally saved them. In his love and pity, he redeemed them and lifted them up and carried them through all the years.

Amy's eyes teared up. "In religion class, we talked about Jesus being 'The Wounded Healer.' This verse describes God's love so well. He became our Savior, and he felt all of our emotions and pain. He understands our afflictions. He knows what it feels like to be human. To think that God even wanted to know what it is like to be human in the first place—wanted to suffer our suffering—is love beyond all measure. Through all of this suffering, he bridges the road between us and eternity. When I feel that people are laughing at me—when I feel jealous and angry—the Lord is with me, wanting to give comfort and guidance. All I have to do is turn to him and ask for his help."

**What emotions have you had that the Wounded Healer has shared with you?**

**Are you able to turn to the Lord easily and ask for his help?**

# May 29

Psalm 66:20 Blessed be God who didn't turn away when I was praying and didn't refuse me his kindness and love.

Amanda Adams thought back on the times she prayed for a precise thing to happen. "My prayers were always heard and answered. Many times the answer was a no, but I eventually saw that my prayer was answered in a more positive way in God's time and God's way. What is comforting to me is that I do know that God does not turn away from me when I pray. And he always gives me his kindness and love. He is always there for me. Many times, though, he didn't really seem to be near me. At times, I have felt abandoned by God. It wasn't God who wasn't near, though. It was me who was distant from God. It was good for me to feel those times of darkness. When the light of God's love turned back on in my heart, I appreciated his brilliant light shining in the darkness so much more.

**Do you feel God's kindness and love when you pray?**

**Have you ever felt the darkness?**


# May 30

Genesis 9:12–15 And I seal this promise with this sign: I have placed my rainbow in the clouds as a sign of my promise until the end of time, to you and to all the earth. When I send clouds over the earth, the rainbow will be seen in the clouds, and I will remember my promise to you and every being, that never again will the floods come and destroy all life.

Sara remembered the story about Noah and the flood. He built a boat to save his family and the animals from the flood. "I love rainbows. I can become a bit scared when a summer thunderstorm comes along. But then the winds calm down, and the rain stops and the sun comes out shining through a beautiful rainbow. I always think of God and His blessings shining through the colors of the rainbow. I feel that God does really care about us and is showing us a sign of his love. I have read stories about finding a pot of gold at the end of a rainbow. I guess that it is really true if you think of God's love being at the end of the rainbow, which is like finding a pot of gold."

**What are your feelings when you see a rainbow?**

**Have you experienced a rainbow appearing in your life after a period of darkness and pain?**

# May 31

Romans 5:3–4 We can rejoice, too, when we run into problems and trials for we know that they are good for us—they help us learn to be patient. And patience develops strength in character in us and helps us trust God more each time we use it until finally our hope and faith are strong and steady.

Sighing, Amy knew this was a true statement St. Paul was making. "Oh, I find it hard to rejoice when problems come my way. I just seem to become more anxious and fearful. Yet, I do think I am beginning to realize that these problems of mine aren't going to last forever. I realize that things and situations do change, and I have indeed learned much. I also can have empathy and reach out to others who are experiencing problems. I am looking forward to the time when I can have a hope and a faith that are strong and steady. I will need God's help in guiding me along the path toward having a strength of character and having a trust in God's love. Please, God, be with me, and guide me. Amen."

**Are you learning to be patient?**

**How do you handle life's trials and problems?**

# 6 June

## June 1

Joel 2:26–27 Praise the Lord, who does these miracles for you. Never again will my people experience disaster such as this. And you will know that I am here among my people Israel, and that I alone am the Lord your God.

Jake had just heard about an earthquake that happened overseas that afternoon. "The quake did a lot of damage and killed many people. It was a true disaster. Many countries are sending in relief teams to find victims under the collapsed buildings. Many volunteers are rushing in to help in whatever way they can. There is a lot of sorrow and suffering taking place, but I know that God is sad. He wants to bring comfort and love to each and every person who has been hit by the earthquake. The volunteers rushing in to help are examples of God working his comfort. When a victim is recovered from under a collapsed building, a miracle has taken place. God's actions are in every person who is trying to help.

**When a disaster came into your life, who was the one God used to help you?**

**Did God give you a feeling of peace in the midst of the disaster?**

# June 2

1 Peter 2:10 Once you were less than nothing; now you are God's own. Once you knew very little of God's kindness; now your very lives have been changed by it.

Jim Adams reflected back on a time when he had drifted away from going to church, and even away from God. "I really didn't know very much about God's kindness. In fact, I didn't really think much about God at all. My feeling was that God didn't really matter much in the scheme of the world. In many respects, a belief in God could get in the way of making my way in the world. It didn't take me long to realize that the world didn't have much to offer except competition, anger, jealousy, addictions and on and on, until I asked if this was all there was. Then God seemed to break through all of my inner turmoil. I surrendered to him and felt peace. I can now live in the world, but with God, I am not of the world. My life has indeed been changed. I no longer feel turmoil. Instead, I feel God's peace."

**Do you live in the world but are not of the world?**

**What does this mean?**

# June 3

1 John 4:7–8 Dear Friends, let us practice loving each other, for love comes from God, and those who are loving and kind show that they are the children of God and that they are getting to know him better. But if a person isn't loving and kind, it shows that he doesn't know God—for God is love.

This verse struck Amy to the center of her heart. "Oh, dear God, I do love you so much. But I find it hard to love, care about, and have compassion for many of the kids at school. When I feel a lack of compassion for others, it shows that I really don't know you, doesn't it, God? I know that I can't will this feeling of compassion for others with my own will power. I need your ever-steady help to guide me along the way. You not only want us to love you and our neighbor, but you want us to care about ourselves as well. Not in a self-centered way, but in a way that we feel a good sense of self-esteem from knowing that you love us. This self-esteem of love then transfers over to other people and over to you also. It is like a triangle of love for you, other people, and for oneself. Thank you, Lord."

**Are you able to love yourself?**

**Do you have a triangle love for God, neighbor, and yourself?**

# June 4

Ephesians 4:2–3 Be humble and gentle. Be patient with each other, making allowance for each other's faults because of your love. Try always to be led along together by the Holy Spirit, and so be at peace with one another.

Sara thought, "That's a pretty thought. It's hard to overlook the faults of the kids at school. There is Fred, who is a bully; Lori, who is a conceited snob; Dora, who likes to tease and put everyone down; and Harry, who is always in trouble. But then how can I make an allowance for them? I guess by trying to understand what makes them act the way they do. Well, I guess Fred doesn't know how to get along with others, so he is a bully. Maybe Lori is just shy and comes across as conceited. Dora hurts others all the time. Maybe she does that because she has been badly hurt herself. And why is Harry always in trouble? Maybe that is the only way he knows how to get attention. I wonder what I do that needs to be understood by others. Holy Spirit, please help me to be at peace with others. Amen."

**Who are the people in your life that need to be understood?**

**How are you able to live in peace with others?**

# June 5

1 Corinthians 3:18–19 Stop fooling yourselves. If you count yourself above average in intelligence, as judged by this world's standards, you had better put this all aside and be a fool rather than let it hold you back from above. For the wisdom of this world is foolishness to God.

Jake thought long and hard about these two verses. "I am graduating from high school tomorrow. Hopefully I do have some intelligence, although I wouldn't say I am above average. What does this verse mean then about having intelligence? Oh, I see, it is intelligence as judged by the world's standards. I think the hardest part is the competition setting one person against another. In every area, including having intelligence, a lot of ego trips go on. God, help me to keep a balance between working to learn the things I need to survive, and yet to still be a part of your kingdom of love and compassion. Amen."

**What wisdom of the world do you think God would consider foolish?**

**What are you above average in that the world admires?**

# June 6

Romans 12:12 Be glad for all God is planning for you. Be patient in trouble and prayerful always.

Amanda Adams read this verse with joyful tears in her eyes. "Jake's high school graduation went so well today. I wish he were here this evening to hear this verse. It is my prayer for him as he leaves this phase of his life and enters a new phase. Life can be much more peaceful when a person chooses to be glad about all the new things that God is planning. How can that peacefulness come about? It comes about by being in constant, heart-filled prayer; by allowing God to be our constant companion; by allowing God to live deep within our hearts; and by knowing that each thought of God during the day can be the deepest kind of prayer. God, protect Jake on this newest phase of his journey. May he allow you to live deeply within his heart. Amen."

**Do you allow God to live deeply within your heart?**

**Do you allow God to be your constant companion?**


# June 7

1 Peter 4:19 So if you are suffering according to God's will, keep on doing what is right and trust yourself to the God who made you, for he will never fail you.

Sara's heart ached as she listened to the verse her mother was reading. "Why did Lottie have to go and shoplift? I will never forget the day when Lottie proudly showed me all the things she had stolen from the stores at the Mall. Oh sure, they were small things, she said, like a tube of lipstick here and a nail file there. But they were adding up. A tiny thing stolen is as bad as a big thing stolen. I had no choice but to tell Lottie that it was wrong to steal. She got so mad at me, and that was the end of our friendship. I miss her and I feel sad. Mom told me to be compassionate and pray for Lottie. I must be firm in telling her that stealing is wrong. I know, God, that you will help me to be strong and to do what is right. Help Lottie realize that stealing is wrong. Help her realize that you love her, but you don't want her to steal. Thank you."

**What have you had to do in standing up for what is right?**

**Have you ever suffered for doing what is right?**

# June 8

Ephesians 4:23–24 Now your attitudes and thoughts must all be constantly changing for the better. Yes, you must be a new and different person, holy and good.

Jim Adams was proud as he watched his oldest child graduate from high school. "Jake is going off to college this fall, and I wonder how he will handle the challenges of his studies and his social life. Will his attitudes change for the better? He is going to face many worldly things, and he will make what might be life long decisions. I, as his dad, fear for him. I pray that Jake will not have to learn things the hard way, but I know I cannot protect him from life. I will continue to put him in your care, God, each day. I trust that you will guide him every step of the way. Jake has the good foundation of your love. I pray that you will continue to give me patience and courage to be a good parent. Amen."

**Are your attitudes changing for the better?**

**Do you feel like you are a new and different person?**

# June 9

Romans 8:26 And in the same way—by our faith—the Holy Spirit helps us with our daily problems and in our praying. For we don't even know what we should pray for, nor how to pray as we should; but the Holy Spirit prays for us with such feeling that it cannot be expressed in words.

Yesterday was a day and a half for Amanda Adams. "When Lois called me yesterday and asked me to have lunch with her, I was thrilled. I had not seen Lois for months. When I arrived at the restaurant and saw Lois, I immediately knew she really needed someone to talk to. I listened to her pour out her tearful heart to me. I agonized with her. I wanted to bring peace and comfort to her, but I realized that only you could do that, God. All I was able to do was just to listen. I had no advice to give her. She did not want any advice, anyway. There are not any easy answers to her problems. All I do know is that the Holy Spirit does pray for us with much feeling. There are not any words that can be expressed for Lois's problems. Holy Spirit, I put Lois in your care. Bless her with your strength and courage. Amen."

**Do you ever pray with your feelings instead of words?**

**Is listening fully to a person a healing gift to give?**

# June 10

1 Corinthians 12:4,7 Now God gives us many kinds of special abilities, but it is the same Holy Spirit who is the source of them all. There are different kinds of service to God, but it is the same Lord we are serving. The Holy Spirit displays God's power through each of us as a means of helping the entire church.

Amanda Adams came close to leaving a group she belonged to at church. "There is a developing feeling of competition in the group. We each take a turn in leading the weekly meeting, but a spirit of competition with a dose of spiritual pride has entered the scene. A feeling of 'my faith is deeper than your faith' is the underlying current in the group. 'My prayers are more beautiful than your prayers,' and 'really, if you were a better Christian, you would want to give more freely of your time to other church activities' are the underlying themes. God, please help us realize that there are different kinds of service to you, but we are all serving the same Lord. Please reunite us by bringing forth love and compassion for each other."

**How do you feel when a bit of spiritual pride enters into your personality?**

**What generally brings you back to feeling a healthy humility?**

# June 11

Ephesians 3:18 And may you be able to feel and understand, as all God's children should, how long, how wide, how deep, and how high his love really is.

"All of my religion education classes this year stressed God's love for us," Amy thought to herself. "I will miss the classes this summer, and yet I am looking forward to spending some lazy days going to the beach and spending time with my friends. I have always taken it for granted that God loves us, but some of my friends have said they do not think God loves us at all. If he did, why did he allow all the bad things that happen in the world take place? Gosh, it is all a mystery to me. I just do not know the answers. However, I do know one thing for sure. God has promised to be with us. We need to ask him to give us the strength to get through and beyond the bad times. He will indeed give us that strength. He loves us deeply. Thank you for your love, God.

**Do you feel God's love and strength during the bad times as well as the good?**

**Did God ever promise us that we would never have any problems?**

# June 12

Colossians 2:8 Don't let others spoil your faith and joy with their philosophies, their wrong and shallow answers built on men's thoughts and ideas instead of on what Christ has said.

"Mom is always saying that we watch too much television," Ted thought to himself. "She really guards the type of programs we watch, and I must admit it makes me pretty mad at times. I guess there are many TV programs that can be a bad influence on all of us. I guess our faith affected is by these negative influences. One TV channel Mom does not allow us to watch is a popular music station. Occasionally, she will let us turn it on. Then she will ask us to talk about what message these songs are giving out. What are these rock groups saying? Sometimes I am embarrassed to have Mom in the room with us, let alone discuss the subject matter. I guess that feeling of embarrassment says it all."

**What are some of the messages you are hearing that could spoil your faith?**

**What steps do we take to improve the music industry?**

# June 13

Galatians 1:10 You can see that I am not trying to please you by sweet talk and flattery; no, I am trying to please God. If I were still trying to please men I could not be Christ's servant.

"This gives me food for thought," sighed Amanda Adams. "What does it mean to be Christ's servant? I guess it means to love God and to love others as we love ourselves. So what then is wrong with trying to please man? We can easily lose sight of God. We might be pleasing others for all the wrong reasons. Are we trying to get people to like us, or do favors for us, or is it to get our own way? However, when we are trying to please God, we want to please others through God's love and not for our own selfish reasons. Therefore, we are then the servant of God, allowing him to do his work through us. I must think and pray about this verse more. Thank you, Lord."

**Do you try to please others through false flattery sweet talk?**

**Do you ever try to manipulate others to get your own way?**

# June 14

1 Peter 2:25 Like sheep you wandered away from God, but now you have returned to your Shepherd, the Guardian of your souls who keeps you safe from all attacks.

Amy just recently realized how much she depended on Jesus to help her fight her anxious, fearful, and jealous feelings. "The other day at the swimming pool, a girl I didn't know came for a swim with friends of mine. Her name was Tina. She was beautiful and had a super personality. I began to feel anxious. I was afraid that she would take my friends away from me. I felt ugly and could not think of a thing to say. I began feeling very jealous. My self-esteem hit bottom. I began feeling a hard dislike for Tina, and I wished she would go away. Then a tiny voice from deep inside my heart reminded me that my negative thinking was back at work. I turned to my Shepherd and prayed 'Lord, please help me work through these negative feelings of mine. Please help me to look at Tina and see her as the beautiful person she is.' A feeling of love and peace came over me. Thank you, Lord, the Shepherd of my heart."

**When do you call on the "Shepherd of your heart" for help?**

**What happens when you get an attack of negative thinking?**

# June 15

James 5:19–20 Dear Brothers, if anyone has slipped away from God and no longer trusts the Lord, and someone helps him understand the truth again, that person who brings him back to God will have saved a wandering soul from death, bringing about the forgiveness of his many sins.

Jim Adams could not help but think about Hank, who had been going through a tough time. "Hank blames all his ill fortune on God. He is so angry with God that I wonder if he will ever come out of his depression. All I can do is pray and be there for Hank if he ever decides to open up and let me into his suffering. I feel so helpless, yet I know that you are with Hank. You care about him more than any of us are capable of caring. I release Hank to your love and care. I will continue to trust you and pray with you that Hank will at last be able to turn away from his anger at you. I pray that he will realize that you love him and that you are not the cause of his misfortune. May Hank heal. May he feel your love. Amen."

**Do you know of anyone who has slipped away from God?**

**What can you do to help that person?**

# June 16

Colossians 1:11–12 We are praying, too, that you will be filled with his mighty, glorious strength so that you can keep going no matter what happens—always full of the joy of the Lord, and always thankful to the Father who has made us fit to share all the wonderful things that belong to those who live in the kingdom of light.

Amanda Adams thought back in her life to when she faced bad times. "I experienced a few bad times before I knew about the strength that God can give. I nearly broke into pieces. I found myself completely feeling out of control with nothing to hold. Then I realized that God was there if only I would turn to him. I found myself turning to the Lord. Since that time, my life has been more peaceful. Each day I turn my life over to God, knowing God, and not me, has the control. There are days when my faith slips, and I wonder if God really cares. Then all I need to do is to look back and see all the positive things God brought forth out of all the negative things that took place."

**Do you believe that God will give you the strength you need during times of trials?**

**Are you able to experience the joy of the Lord even in the trials of life?**

# June 17

Hebrews 13:5–6 Stay away from the love of money; be satisfied with what you have. For God has said, "I will never, never fail you nor forsake you." That is why we can say without any doubt or fear, "The Lord is my helper and I am not afraid of anything that mere man can do to me."

"How do I feel about money?" Jake asked himself. "In September I will start my first year of college. I must ask myself what I will do with my education. Will I use it for the making of a great deal of money? Or will I use my education to help others who are less fortunate than me? Will I use my education to compete and step over people who get in my way? On the other hand, will I use it to be a generous, honest person who cares about the people he works with? If I am satisfied with what I have at any given time, then I will not be tempted to compete by walking over other people on my way to the so-called top. God, I know you are my helper. I know that I do not need to be afraid of what I may do to others as well as what others can do to me."

**Do you have an over abundant love of money, security, popularity or anything else that can come between you and God?**

**Do you know that God will guide you in being an honest person?**

# June 18

James 2:1 Dear Brother, how can you claim that you belong to the Lord Jesus Christ, the Lord of glory, if you show favoritism to rich people and look down on poor people?

Sara felt her face grow red. "I looked down on Karen the other day at the park. Oh, I'm so sorry, God. Karen's family just moved here from another state. They do not talk like us, and they don't dress like us. Mom has insisted that I make friends with Karen, but she embarrasses me. I do not want my friends to see me with her. This is not nice of me, is it, God? Karen is a real nice girl who is fun. I just wish she were not so different from the rest of us. Mom asked me how I would feel if I moved to Karen's hometown and her friends did not want to be around me because I was different. I would not like it. God, please help me to overcome this feeling of mine. Help me be a true friend to Karen."

**Have you ever felt different from the rest of the crowd?**

**How do you treat those who are different from you?**

# June 19

1 Peter 8–9 You love him even though you have never seen him; though not seeing him, you trust him; and even now you are happy with the inexpressible joy that comes from heaven itself. And your further reward for trusting him will be the salvation of your souls.

Ted had been bored with church. "I'm even bored with this after dinner ritual of Mom and Dad reading scripture every evening. I want to get back outdoors and on to baseball practice. Yet deep down, I know that as each day passes, I am getting to know about God more and more. I am not able to see him, but he does come alive in the scripture and at church. Because of all of this, even though I am bored with it all, I know that it is helping me to believe and to trust in God without ever seeing him. Heck, I bet God likes to play a good game of baseball, too, so I will take him with me, and that too can be my prayer. After all, Mom and Dad say God is at our side at all times."

**Have you ever gotten bored with church?**

**What was the outcome of this boredom?**

# June 20

Matthew 9:12–13 "Because people who are well don't need a doctor! It is the sick people who do!" was Jesus' reply! Then he added, "Now go away and learn the meaning of this verse of scripture, 'It isn't your sacrifices and your gifts I want—I want you to be merciful.' for I have come to urge sinners, not the self-righteous, back to God."

Amanda Adams needed to read these verses occasionally to remind her that she was not to become self-righteous. "Every so often I will meet someone at church who I find lacking in what I feel makes up the characteristics of a 'good Christian.' The feeling of self-righteousness is so insidious. It creeps in without my even being aware of it. I realize that church is for healing those wounds of being human. It is there for the wounded as well as for the righteous. Who is to say when something will come along and pull the rug of our self-righteousness right out from under our smug, all knowing ways? God, please help me reach out to those people who are so wounded and in need of your love."

**Have you ever judged others as not being good Christians?**

**What does God mean that he just wants us to be merciful?**

# June 21

Luke 5:1–3 One day as he was preaching on the shore of Lake Gennesaret, great crowds pressed in on him to listen to the Word of God. We noticed two empty boats standing at the water's edge while the fishermen washed their nets. Stepping into one of the boats, Jesus asked Simon, its owner, to push out a little into the water so that he could sit in the boat and speak to the crowds from there.

"Wow!" thought Ted to himself. "What would I think if this man came up to me while I was washing my nets and stepped into my boat without my permission? Then he asks me to push the boat out a little so he could sit in my boat. He said he wanted to speak to the crowds that were gathering around us. I'd probably be a little upset because I would want to get my nets cleaned up. After all, fishing would be my business. I probably would not have patience for this man and for all the crowds that were following him. I wonder if I would feel like that, even though I am not a fisherman. How many times do people ask me to do things for God and I find it inconvenient to do so? God, open my eyes. Amen."

**Do you make the time for Christ to use your boat?**

**How much time do you spend on becoming a patient person?**

# June 22

Psalm 103:8–9 He is merciful and tender toward those who don't deserve it; He is slow to get angry and full of kindness and love. He never bears a grudge, nor remains angry forever.

"I wish I could be like God in this one particular way," Amy thought. "I find that I am always getting angry at someone. I am so sensitive to what other people say or do; therefore, I am quick to take offense. Then I become angry, and I bear a grudge against that person. Does this anger and grudge holding bring me peace? No, God, why am I so sensitive to what others are saying and doing? Why do I take things so personally? I need to let things roll off my back. Why do I take each word into my mind and measure its content? Actually, God, this being sensitive to what others say does not show love toward them. Help me overcome this weakness. Help me to be slow to anger, and to be full of kindness and love. Amen."

**Do you hold grudges?**

**If so, what does holding a grudge do to your outlook on life?**

# June 23

Psalm 84:5–6 Happy are those who are strong in the Lord, who want above all else to follow your steps. When they walk through the Valley of Weeping it will become a place of springs where pools of blessing and refreshment collect after rains!

Amanda Adams thought that she should memorize these two verses." This is the foundation of the Lord's love for us. When I truly want to follow God's steps—wanting to love him, to love others, and to love myself—I am doing God's will. When I know how much God loves me and how much he wants me to live life abundantly, then I learn to trust him. When things go wrong, and living life on this earth will indeed bring inner suffering, then God is with us in the suffering if we allow him into our hearts. Through our tears, we will come to God's pools of blessing and refreshment. We will find rest in our tears. We will find courage and love and strength through God's love for us."

**Do you feel that you are strong in the Lord?**

**Have you ever come to see God's pools of refreshment and blessings through the Valley of Weeping?**

# June 24

Luke 7:47 "Therefore her sins—and they are many—are forgiven, for she loved me much; but one who is forgiven little, shows little love."

"Hey!" Jake thought, "What does this verse mean? Here is a woman who sinned a lot, and Jesus forgives her because she loves him a lot. Oh, I see. When someone who sins realizes how wrong he has been and turns to Jesus, the person's sins are forgiven. The person who loves Jesus will realize what his sins are and will try not to repeat them. However, the person who keeps all the rules and regulations, and who begins to feel a spiritual pride because he does keep the rules, is not a loving or a forgiving person. He becomes self-righteous and condemning. When that happens, there isn't a love for Jesus, but instead a love for rules and regulations, which brings on spiritual pride and pettiness."

**Have you ever been self-righteous?**

**If so, were you a very loving person?**

# June 25

Psalm 69:13 But I keep right on praying to you, Lord. For now is the time—you are bending down to hear! You are ready with a plentiful supply of love and kindness.

Sally loved bedtime. "Mommie and Daddy like for me to say my prayers before going to bed. I ask you, God, to take care of everyone, and Ginger, and the squirrels, and the birds. I like the book of stories about you read to me. I used to have nightmares once in awhile, but now that I say my night prayers to you, I am not afraid anymore. I know that besides Mommie and Daddy watching out for me, you are looking after all of us. Mommie says you love me very much. You love all of us an awful lot. Daddy says that you are very kind and you care about what happens to us. I will keep on praying to you every night, God, because I like to."

**Do you feel like God is bending down to hear your prayers?**

**How did you feel about bedtime when you were little?**

# June 26

John 4:13–14 Jesus replied that people soon became thirsty again after drinking this water. "But the water I give them," he said, "becomes a perpetual spring within them, watering them forever with eternal life."

"I've been feeling down the past few days," thought Amanda Adams to herself. "I really don't have any reason to feel blue that I know of. When I get these depressed feelings, God generally seems far away, although I know deep within my heart that he is very near and is with me in my depression. I think many people have the mistaken idea that a Christian should never feel blue. If a person is doing God's will, he should be feeling wonderfully happy. I find, though, that my depressed feelings are a time of spiritual growth for me. I certainly do not like the depressed feelings, but they call for a test of faith on my part. They ask me if I love God for who he is, or do I love God for all the good things he can give me? It takes a true faith to love God in the midst of down times. My comfort is that my true friend is at my side."

**How do you feel about God during the down times?**

**When has God seemed to be far away?**

# June 27

Romans 5:20 Ten Commandments were given so that all could see the extent of their failure to obey God's laws. But the more we see our sinfulness, the more we see God's abounding grace forgiving us.

Sara remembered Mrs. Lewis talking about the Ten Commandments in her religion class. "At first I felt scared that God would be mad at me for doing something wrong and punish me. Then Mrs. Lewis talked to us about God giving us the grace to recognize our sins. I asked Mrs. Lewis what a sin was. She said doing anything against the Ten Commandments was a sin. She said a good rule to follow in keeping all the Commandments was to love God with your heart, mind, and soul, and to love your neighbor as yourself. If you do this, you will be free of sin. She suggested that we pray daily, asking God to guide us because we need his help. We need his grace. We need God's help in following the Ten Commandments. Thank you, God, for your understanding love and guidance. Amen."

**Do you remember when you first heard about the Ten Commandments?**

**What was your reaction?**

# June 28

Galatians 5:4–15 For the whole Law can be summed up in this one command: "Love others as you love yourself." But if instead of showing love among yourselves you are always critical and catty, watch out! Beware of ruining each other.

Amanda Adams sighed to herself. "Lately a group of people at church has become very critical of the ways things are being managed at church. There seems to be an air of competition of who can organize the best prayer service, put together the best church social, or who can belong to the most church organizations. It is getting so bad that there is even competition as to who can look and act the most holy. I have noticed many catty remarks being said. The atmosphere has become very tense. It has happened so fast. What once was a loving, encouraging community has become a back biting, tearing down, competitive community. God, please help all of us realize that instead of building up our community, we are ruining each other. Help us, God. Thank you. Amen."

**What can you do to repair damage done by lack of love and respect for each other?**

**Why do people fall into the trap of doing their will in God's name?**


# June 29

Philippians 2:14–16 In everything you do, stay away from complaining and arguing, so that no one can speak a word of blame against you. You are to live clean, innocent lives as children of God in a dark world full of people who are crooked and stubborn. Shine out among them like beacon light, holding out to them the Word of Life.

Jim Adams also had noticed the changes in the church community. "Now that the summer vacations are taking place, there seems to be a lessening of the spiritual pride I noticed last spring. It is always a surprise to acknowledge that people who attend church can become much like the people out there in the world. I know that our Pastor realizes what is going on. Some people who are caught up in this religious competition are going through another phase of faith development. Spiritual pride is a pitfall for a Christian who begins to feel self-righteous; that he has arrived and found the one true way to God. When the Christian realizes that God reaches each of us in an unique way, and in his own time, the spiritual pride will be gone. The realization will come that when we think we have 'arrived,' we are in trouble."

**Give some examples of spiritual pride.**

**How has God worked in your life in an unique way?**

# June 30

1 Timothy 4:7 Don't waste time arguing over foolish ideas and silly myths and legends. Spend your time and energy in the exercise of keeping spiritually fit.

Jake loved exercising. "I run every morning before breakfast, but I never thought about keeping spiritually fit. I wonder if I began talking to God while I am running would be a good way to keep spiritually fit? I bet it would. Mom says that God is always with us, so we can talk to him at all times. She says we need the church community as well in giving us God's support. Boy, what I've seen lately with the adults in the community is something else. They do seem to waste time arguing about this, that, or the other. Dad says it is just a phase in the spiritual maturity of the community. He suggested I look at it, learn from it, and pray for the healing of the many wounds that are taking place. God, I pray that you will lead me in the ways of keeping spiritually fit."

**In what ways do you keep spiritually fit?**

**What is spiritual maturity?**

 July

# July 1

2 Timothy 2:16–17 Steer clear of foolish discussions, which lead people into the sin of anger with each other. Things will be said that will burn and hurt for a long time to come.

This verse really hit home for Amy. "Oh, God, how true it is. St. Paul is right in his advice about steering clear of foolish discussions, particularly when it comes to religious beliefs. I wish I could take my words back, which I know hurt my friend, Liz. She attends another church in town, and we got on to discussing the differences in our two religions. Before I knew it, I told her that her religion was wrong in their beliefs. They were not following the true way to God. Liz was furious with me. She called me a self-righteous religious bigot who had no love or understanding for anyone but my own kind. Oh, God, I failed to give my love and understanding to Liz. Our friendship will never be the same again. Here we both love you, and I failed to recognize that there are many paths leading to you. I'm so sorry, God."

**Can you remember any foolish discussions that brought on anger in your life?**

**Have you ever met a self–righteous person who felt his way was the only way?**

# July 2

1 John 4:11–12 Dear Friends, since God loved us as much as that, we surely ought to love each other, too. For though we have never yet seen God, when we love each other, God lives in us, and his love within us grows ever stronger.

Sally yawned as Mom read from scripture. "There are so many big words that I don't understand. I had fun at Vacation Bible School this week. Mrs. Lowe told us that Jesus loves us very much. Because he loves each of us, we then should love each other. I told Mrs. Lowe that I could not see how Jesus could possibly love Eddie. He is a bully. I cannot stand him. Mrs. Lowe then told me that Jesus loves Eddie very much, just as Jesus loves me very much. I said that I would try to love Eddie, but I sure did not like him being a bully. Mrs. Lowe said that I did not have to like what Eddie did. In fact, I should pray for Eddie, asking God to help Eddie find love and kindness deep within his heart. God, I am praying to you that you will help Eddie, and that you will help me to love Eddie. Amen."

**Have you ever had a bully enter your life?**

**What was your reaction?**


# July 3

1 Corinthians 3:3 When you are jealous of one another and divide up into quarreling groups, doesn't that prove you are still babies, wanting your own way? In fact, you are acting like people who do not belong to the Lord at all.

Ted thought back to a Sunday last spring when he overheard a group of people talking about the church service the children of the community were in charge of that day. "I heard Mrs. Core talking about what she felt was a disrespect shown by the readers of the scriptures that morning. Gosh, I was one of the readers. I really practiced, but I was so nervous I goofed up. Often adults do not understand a person making a mistake. Then Mr. Core said he could not understand the need to waste the adults' worship time by turning the service over to a bunch of kids to be in charge. Next time he was going to make it a point to go to another church on children's Sunday. God, why do people act that way? Is it because they are actually still babies wanting their own way? Mom told me to pray that Mr. & Mrs. Core will learn to love others as well as loving you, God."

**Have your ever encountered a Mr. and Mrs. Core in your church community?**

**Do critical complaining people bring peace and blessing to any group?**


# July 4

Psalm 28:9 Defend your people, Lord; defend and bless your chosen ones. Lead them like a Shepherd and carry them forever in your arms.

Jim Adams prayed silently, "Yes, Lord, please defend us. Bless this country and the people in it. The foundation of our country is God, liberty, and religious freedom. During the past two hundred years, we have gone from one extreme to another, trying to maintain a balance of governing laws and religious freedom. We have now gone too far in the direction of too much freedom. The government is becoming the fix it all, the problem solver. The government is becoming man's religion, it seems. God, help us keep the balance between the government and religion. Help us to maintain our religious values of knowing right from wrong. Help us regain hope. We are discovering that government cannot solve all the problems. We need government and religion working hand in hand together."

**Do you feel our country is on the right path?**

**Where do you feel we are out of balance?**

# July 5

Isaiah 40:6–8 Shout that man is like the grass that dies away, and all his beauty fades like dying flowers. The grass withers, and the flower fade beneath the breath of God. And so it is with fragile man. The grass withers, the flowers fade, but the Word of our God shall stand forever.

Jim Adams broke the silence of the quiet time and said, "The grass withers, the flowers fade, but the Word of our God shall stand forever." Jim then closed his eyes and prayed silently. "Father, please remind me that we are only in this world a very short time. I do not know what you want me to do in this world except to love you, to love others, and to love myself. You give each of us gifts for building your kingdom but they are not our gifts for our own personal use. Generally, we are unaware of how you work through each of us to reach out to others in love and compassion. We humans are frail, and we will pass from this earth. It is comforting to know that although we will pass from the earth; your Word will live on."

**In what ways has God given you love and comfort?**

**Do you keep in mind that we are only in this world a very short time?**

# July 6

Isaiah 40:27–28 O Jacob, O Israel, how can you say that the Lord doesn't see your trouble and isn't being fair? Don't you yet understand? Don't you know by now that the everlasting God, the creator of the farthest parts of the earth, never grows faint or weary? No one can fathom the depths of his understanding.

"How beautiful," Amanda Adams thought as she read these two verses. "How many times have I felt or said how unfair life can be? Does God realize how much suffering goes on in the world? Is he so indifferent to us? He does understand, and no—none of us can possibly fathom the depths of his understanding. We are not able to see the big picture as God can. We only see the bits and pieces. So much about God is a mystery to us. Moreover, the hardest part for us is to accept the mystery and to have a deep faith that all will be well. We need to trust that God does love us, cares about us, and understands us. Help me to believe. Help my faith."

**Do you feel that God sees your troubles?**

**Why is it so hard to fathom the depth of God's understanding?**

# July 7

Isaiah 40:29–31 He gives power to the tired and worn out, and strength to the weak. Even the youths shall be exhausted, and the young men will all give up. But they that wait upon the Lord shall renew their strength. They shall mount up with wings like eagles; they shall run and not be weary; they shall walk and not faint.

"Man, that's encouraging!" sighed Jake. "All we have to do is wait for the Lord to renew our strength. I hope I will remember this when I am bogged down with my studies at college this fall. I am somewhat concerned about how well I will do in school. Some of my friends who just finished their first year at college did not do very well. They made it, but only by a narrow margin. They admitted they had trouble adjusting to working their study time in with the social time. In addition, their college courses were much harder than their high school classes. God, please give me the strength and the discipline to succeed in college."

**Have there been times when you felt exhausted and weary?**

**What brought you renewed energy?**

# July 8

Philippians 4:12–13 I know how to live on almost nothing or with everything. I have learned the secret of contentment in every situation, whether it be a full stomach or hunger, plenty or want for I can do everything God asks me to with the help of Christ who gives me the strength and power.

"That is the secret of feeling peace in the life." Jim Adams had been struggling with an inner turmoil concerning a possible change in his job. "I've been feeling so restless lately. If only I could learn to live on almost nothing, or else with everything. I guess that is why I like to take the family camping. It gets us away from all the conveniences of modern life and shows us we can indeed survive on very little. Life becomes simple once again. Well, God, if I must have a change come at work, then I ask you, Christ, to give me the strength and the power to make the transition. Please teach me the secret of feeling content in every situation. What a freedom the feeling of contentment in any situation would give to our souls."

**Are you able to feel content in every situation?**

**Do you like to go camping?**

# July 9

2 Corinthians 9:6–7 But remember this—if you give little, you will get little. A farmer who plants just a few seeds will get only a small crop, but if he plants much, he will reap much.

What a wonderful day this has been!" Sara was thinking about the drive to the State Park they made for a week of camping. "On our trip here, I saw the fields of corn and the results of all the work the farmers had done. Well, I am not a farmer, who plants seeds, so how does this story apply to me? Oh, I know. When we arrived at the campsite, I was really somewhat tired. I did not want to help set up the tent and unpack the car, so I made a fuss. I ended up sitting down away from the fun the rest of the family was having. I felt left out, because I did not want to help. I gave little and received little. It almost ruined what had been a near perfect day. I am glad I said I was sorry and then offered to wash the dishes. I could then share the fun we were having as a family unit."

**Have there been times you gave little?**

**What were the results?**

# July 10

2 Corinthians 9:7 Every one must make up his own mind as to how much he should give. Don't force anyone to give more than he really wants to, for cheerful givers are the ones God prizes.

"I wonder if Mom read this verse on purpose. I sense a lecture here," thought Amy. "I do like camping, but I sure would like some conveniences, too. I get tired of carrying water to the campsite. I wish Dad would find a campsite with water on it. We get tired of carrying water to our site. I want Dad to find a site with electricity.

Well, at least we do have a bathhouse with electricity so I can blow dry my hair. I do not think God prizes me much today because I have not been a very cheerful giver. In fact, everything is getting on my nerves. Okay, God, I must make up my own mind about how much I want to give. I cannot do this on my own. I need your help because frankly, I do not even want to be here. God, please give me the patience and the strength to find joy and contentment for the sake of the family."

**Are you a cheerful giver?**

**If not, how do you handle the situation?**

# July 11

Ephesians 2:14 For Christ himself is our way of peace. He has made peace between us Jews and you Gentiles by making us all one family, breaking down the wall of contempt that used to separate us.

Ted thought about the bickering that went on all day between Amy and Sara. "I guess I was part of the bickering, too. The problem is that Dad insists that we camp at a site that does not have electricity and water. We kids are expected to go after the water, and with no electricity, there is not any TV. It is so boring. Anyway, we are acting like the Jews and the Gentiles. A wall of contempt is separating us. I pray that you will bring a change of attitude in us, Jesus. This is supposed to be a fun time for us as a family, and each of us has a selfish, I-don't-want-to-do-anything attitude that is making us all miserable. Help us work together to bring about family cooperation."

**Do you feel Christ is your way toward peace?**

**Do you have a wall of contempt that needs to be broken down?**

# July 12

Psalm 91:4–6 He will shield you with his wings! They well shelter you. His faithful promises are your armor. Now you do not need to be afraid of the dark anymore, nor fear the dangers of the day; nor dread the plagues of darkness, nor disasters in the morning.

"I like camping, and I am having a good time, but I am so afraid of the dark," Sally brooded to herself. "The tent is so dark. I woke up in the middle of the night last night and realized that everyone else was asleep. I was the only one awake. It scared me. Mom heard me crying and told me that God was awake, and he was watching over us. She told me that I did not need to be afraid. Mom told me to trust that God would take good care of us. I guess that is the truth. It is not really so scary, and I am having so much fun here. Amy and Jake took me swimming today while Ted and Sara went fishing with Dad. I like the swimming pool here at the park. Amy and Jake are trying to teach me how to swim. Thank you, God, for my family and the fun I am having here camping."

**Do you feel that God is shielding you with his wings?**

**Are God's faithful promises your armor?**

# July 13

2 Corinthians 6:3–4 We try to live in such a way that no one will ever be offended or kept back from finding the Lord by the way we act, so that no one can find fault with us and blame it on the Lord. In fact, in everything we do we try to show that we are true ministers of God.

Amanda Adams was relieved that this was the first day that the family camping trip had gone well. "Everyone had a good time today. I am sure that you, God, are proud of us. You answered our prayers with a big yes when we asked for help with our attitudes. I think the children finally have come to realize that we really do not need all of our modern conveniences to make us happy. It is all a matter of our attitude towards life. Either we have a choice to make do with what we have, or we can decide not to enjoy the things we do have. I know that we need your help, God, in giving us positive attitudes. I now thank you for the gift of a beautiful day, brought on by the gift of beautiful attitudes."

**Do you know how to make do with what you have?**

**Is your attitude about life positive or negative?**


# July 14

2 Corinthians 13:5 Check up on yourselves. Are you really Christians? Do you pass the test? Do you feel Christ's presence, power more, and more within you? Or are you just pretending to be Christians when actually you aren't at all?

It was the last night of camping, and Jim Adams was sorry the vacation was nearly over. "We started out pretty rocky. The first couple of days were tense, but finally everyone caught the spirit of the adventure of camping. Prayer helped, that is for sure! If we check up on ourselves, are we really Christians? Do we feel Christ's presence, power more, and more within us? Yes. Without God's presence, I really believe this camping vacation would have been a disaster. With God's help, we were able to cooperate with each other. We then enjoyed the vacation as a family and individually as well. Thank you, God, for making this a vacation we will always remember."

**Check up on yourself. Are you really a Christian?**

**Do you feel Christ's presence in your life?**

# July 15

Galatians 6:4–5 Let everyone be sure that he is doing his very best, for then he will have the personal satisfaction of work well done, and won't need to compare himself with someone else. All of us must bear some faults and burdens of our own, for none of us is perfect.

Jake was relieved that the camping trip had gone as well as it had. "I'm glad to be back home. I can truly say I did my best on the family vacation. I guess I know that this was the last vacation with the whole family, and I really wanted it to go well. We all acted up in one way or another, and each of us has faults. None of us is perfect. However, we love each other, and we accept each other as we are. God gives us the gift of acceptance and love. Thank you, God, for giving us a special memory of our family vacation. You love us unconditionally, and you helped us love each other with compassionate understanding."

**Do you feel that you are doing your very best?**

**In what ways do you need to improve?**

# July 16

Romans 1:22 Claiming themselves to be wise without God, they became utter fools instead.

"Wow! Those are sobering words!" Jim Adams exclaimed. "Just look around at our secular world and you will see fools everywhere. Watch the newscasts on TV and see a lesson on being a fool. We go from one disaster or problem to another, pointing fingers, and never really come up with solutions. Maybe there are not any solutions if we do not bring God into our everyday lives. Moreover, what would bring God into our lives do to solve the world's problems? Well, if we begin with loving God and loving others—and yes, loving our-selves as well—the world would begin to be healed. If each one of us started bringing the kingdom of God to the hearts of others and our communities, the kingdom of God would ripple out into the world. Without God's help, we will never be wise. Unfortunately, most of us do not open up to receive God's help. So, the world is foolish because we are foolish."

**Do you listen to what God is saying?**

**If not, are you a fool?**


# July 17

Colossians 2:6 And now just as you trusted Christ to save you, trust him too, for each day's problems, live in vital union with him.

Amanda Adams remembered being a child when she first heard about Christ saving people. "I didn't understand about what it meant to be saved. As I became an adult, I began to understand that I could trust Christ to save me from my sins. Then I came to terms with my shopping lists of sins. They were nothing more than symp-toms of negative thinking and low self-esteem. The sins were of a deep anger and a negative, clinging pride. This is what I could do to trust Jesus to save me. I could trust him to guide me on the journey toward letting go of my destructive faults. I came to trust him and rely on him in helping me with my daily problems. I did this by living in union with him; by turning my life and my will over to him; by realizing that the journey towards wholeness is a process of living one day at a time."

**Are you able to trust the Lord to help you with your day-to-day problems?**

**Do you thank him each day for his help?**

# July 18

Ephesians 2:9 Salvation is not a reward for the good we have done, so none of us can take any credit for it.

Amy thought of her friend at church who seemed to be so self-righteous. "Julie acts like she is so holy. She really looks down her nose at the rest of us because we do not know scripture as she does. She has even said that we 'have not been saved' because we do not act very religious. I know that Julie's family is very religious, and they try very hard to do good things, but there is something missing. When I am around Julie and her family, I tend to feel bad about myself. I do not feel like Julia loves or cares about me, other than to check to see if I am doing the holy things, she thinks everyone should do. Jesus saves me because he is leading me to do loving things towards others and myself. How can I love Julie? I can care about her, understand her, and ask God to help me feel compassion towards her."

**Do you feel that salvation is a reward for being good?**

**Can we really be good without God's help?**

# July 19

2 Corinthians 12:9 Each time he said, "No, but I am with you; that is all you need. My power shows up best in weak people." Now I am glad to boast about how weak I am; I am glad to be a living demonstration of Christ's power of showing off my own power and abilities.

"It's hard for me to realize that St. Paul, just like me, had weaknesses," thought Jim Adams. "I grew up thinking that St. Paul had it all together. What a comfort it is to know that he did have weaknesses, which he allowed God to work through in reaching out to others. It is because of my own weakness that I am able to keep in mind how much I truly need God's help. My weakness keeps me honest and keeps my life in proper prospective. I need God's help in everything I do. The minute I think I can do something with my own power without God's help, I fall flat on my face. I thank you, God, for the wisdom you have given me in realizing I can't do your will without your guidance."

**What are your weaknesses?**

**How does God's power show up through your weakness?**

# July 20

1 Peter 2:1 So get rid of your feelings of hatred. Do not just pretend to be good! Be done with dishonesty and jealousy and talking about others behind their backs.

Amy sighed to herself, "O boy, when am I going to stop talking about others behind their backs? Just this morning I found myself feeling angry at Nan for not inviting me to a party she is giving this weekend. So what did I do? I talked to Mary and Delores about Nan. She is selfish for not inviting the three of us to her party. We really tore Nan up. Then this afternoon, I saw Nan at the shopping center. She told me that she was going to have a party and she wanted Mary, Delores, and me to come. I felt awful for talking about her behind her back. I had been jealous of her and hurt, and I jumped to the conclusion that she was not going to invite me to her party. I felt that she thought she was too good for me. Oh, God, I am sorry. Nan has always been nice to me. Why do I want to strike out at her? Please help me with this terrible weakness of jealousy."

**Do you ever talk about others behind their backs?**

**What do you think motivates you to do so?**

# July 21

Matthew 10:29–31 Not one sparrow (What do they cost? Two for a Penny?) can fall to the ground without your Father knowing it. And the very hairs of your head are all numbered. So don't worry! You are more valuable to him than many sparrows.

Sally tried to remember what a sparrow looked like. "I remember Mommie pointing it out to me in my book about birds. I saw sparrows in our yard. They aren't as pretty as some of the other birds like the red birds or the blue birds, or even the robins. There seem to be more sparrows than the other kinds of birds. Gosh, God knows what even these little sparrows are doing. If he knows about sparrows, then he must really care about us and know everything about us, too. I wonder if God cares about bugs, too. Does he care about what an ant is doing? I bet he does. Mom says that God made everything in this world; even the plants, the sun, and the moon, too. She says God loves all of his creation. It's nice to know that God loves us so much."

**Do you believe that God has counted every hair on your head?**

**Isn't it wonderful being part of God's creation?**

# July 22

Roman 15:5 May God who gives patience, steadiness, and encouragement help you to live in complete harmony with each other—each with the attitude of Christ toward the other.

Jake had really been on edge since coming home from the family camping trip. "I'm anxious to get on to college. I must admit I am feeling nervous. Am I going to do well, or am I going to fall flat on my face? I sure haven't shown any patience with the family. Even Ginger gets on my nerves. I think she can sense that I am uptight.

She wants to be with me. She follows me everywhere, and that bugs me. I can't even stand myself. God, I ask you to give me patience, steadiness, and yes, encouragement, too. I want to live in harmony with everyone. I know my being so short-tempered hurts others. I don't want to be hard to get along with. Maybe I should admit that I am nervous about college, and that's why I've been acting like a pill. God, please encourage me to be a caring person."

**At what times have you felt God giving you patience, steadiness, and encouragement.**

**What makes you feel anxious?**

# July 23

Romans 14:1, 4 Give a warm welcome to any brother who wants to join you, even though his faith is weak. Don't criticize him for having different ideas from yours about what is right and wrong. They are God's servants, not yours. They are responsible to him, not to you. Let him tell them whether they are right or wrong. And God is able to make them do as they should.

"Amen to that," Amanda Adams sighed to herself. "I don't know what is going on with Harriet anymore. Our scripture study group is becoming a chore because of Harriet. A number of new people have come into the group, and she doesn't like it one bit. She feels that they don't know scripture at all, and the little they do know, she criticizes as being wrong. It's embarrassing. Actually, the new people bring a new freshness and a new awareness to our scripture study. I wonder if Harriet feels threatened since we have allowed her to be the so-called expert in our group. Maybe the time has come for her to stop being the expert. God, please guide us."

**How do you react to new people coming into your life?**

**What don't you like about change?**

# July 24

Psalm 25:15–17 My eyes are ever looking to the Lord for help, for he alone can rescue me. Come, Lord, and show me your mercy, for I am helpless, overwhelmed, in deep distress; my problems go from bad to worse. Oh, save me from them all!

Amy silently cried to herself as she heard Jake read this verse. "God, please help me. I do feel so helpless, so overwhelmed. I try so hard to do my best, but my best isn't good enough. I was so excited about my school nominating me for the summer program at the art school. Today when I went to register, I was told that the artwork I submitted wasn't as good as the other work submitted by my competition. My nomination was turned down. God, I hurt so much. I don't have any talents. Now the one thing I thought I could do fairly well has also been taken away. I can't even draw. What can I do? I feel so blue. God, please bring me comfort. I hurt so much." As Amy sat and listened to the quiet, she felt a calm peace come over her. Her inner voice said, "All is well. Live each day at a time. A beautiful talent will develop that you will not be aware of, but that others will cherish."

**When have you felt helpless and overwhelmed?**

**How do you handle life's disappointments?**

# July 25

Colossians 3:13 Be gentle and ready to forgive; never hold grudges. Remember, the Lord forgave you, so you must forgive others.

"I wish I could be gentle," Ted sighed to himself. "It seems like I am always losing my temper. If I control my temper, then I sit on my anger and find myself holding a grudge against the person

I am angry with. God, I need to learn how to express my anger in a controlled, mature way. I know it is okay to be angry, but it isn't okay to lose my temper or to hold grudges. God, I want to be a gentle, forgiving person, but I am not able to do this on my own. I need your help. I guess at the bottom of my temper is a feeling that I don't measure up. When I feel threatened, I blow up. I guess I just don't feel good about myself. Am I measuring my worth by trying to live up to what I think the world wants me to be, or do I measure my worth by what you want me to be? I want to be what you want me to be, God. Please guide me."

**Do you measure your worth by God's standards, or by the world's standards?**

**Do you ever lose your temper?**

# July 26

James 5:11 Job is an example of a man who continued to trust the Lord in sorrow; from his experience we can see how the Lord's plan finally ended in good, for he is full of tenderness and mercy.

Amanda Adams wondered how Job continued to trust the Lord in the midst of all his sorrow. "I wonder how I would react if I lost everything. The thought frightens me. I don't think I could be patient and trusting like Job. I believe I would have to beg the Lord to help me trust. I have had just enough sorrow to have experienced the pain of grieving. Sorrow is an overwhelming feeling of the loss of control and the knowledge of just how fragile we humans are. After experiencing all these emotions, it was my utter despair that brought me back to the Lord. His love, his peace, and his healing flowed over me. Step by step, I began to feel hope once again. The only salvation in the midst of despair is trusting the Lord like Job trusted God."

**Do you believe that God is full of tenderness and mercy?**

**Have you ever experienced a despairing loss?**

# July 27

Psalm 44:23–26 Waken! Rouse yourself! Don't sleep, O Lord! Are we cast off forever? Why do you look the other way? Why do you ignore our sorrows and oppression? We lay face downward in the dust. Rise up, O Lord, and come and help us. Save us by your constant love.

"Since getting back from vacation, things haven't been going well at work," Jim Adams thought wearily. "The company just isn't the same now that we are under new management. I don't know the name of the game is anymore. I keep guessing, but I seem to guess the wrong answer. I've tried to talk to our new manger, but we don't seem to come in on the same wavelength. I am beginning to think I am going to have to look for a new job, and the thought frightens me. I sense that the new manager would like us old timers to leave, but they won't fire us. Instead, they will encourage us to leave. God, I have asked for your help, and I must have faith that things will work out okay. Perhaps I do need to look for a new job. If so, please help me, encourage me, affirm me, and give me the strength to move on and grow."

**Have you ever felt that you were cast off forever?**

**What happened? How did God help you?**

# July 28

Isaiah 41:10 Fear not, for I am with you. Do not be dismayed. I am your God. I will strengthen you; I will help you; I will uphold you with my victorious right hand.

Sara was enjoying her summer vacation. "I enjoy reading so much, God. I love going to the library and finding new books to read. I don't have any friends to pal around with this summer, and that makes me feel sad. Yet there are times when I find that I enjoy reading far more than being with the other kids. I wonder if there is something wrong with me. I like the kids, but I don't feel like I fit in with them. They are loud and pushy, and they tease me because I am quiet and I don't talk much. I feel like there is something wrong with me because I don't act like them. Mommie and Daddy have stressed to us that it is important to be polite and caring towards others. But you know what, God? I am treated badly by the kids because they think I am weird. God, will you give me strength to continue to do what is right? Yes, God, I know you are with me. You are helping me. Thank you."

**Have you every felt left out of a group of people?**

**How did God help you?**

# July 29

Romans 8:38 For I am convinced that nothing can ever separate us from his love. Death can't, and life can't. The angels won't, and all the powers of hell itself cannot keep God's love away.

"What a beautiful reading." Amanda Adams remembered an aunt of hers who talked about the wrath of God and his judgment. "Aunt Hilda was a very unhappy and bitter woman. She used to scare me to death with her stories about God's punishment. She told me that whenever I did something bad, it would be added to the list being kept by God. She told me that God would punish me. Despite Aunt Hilda's stories, I knew that God had a deep love for each of us. God loved Aunt Hilda also, even though she seemed to view him as mean and vengeful. Somewhere along the line, someone or something must have hurt Aunt Hilda very much. Maybe someone told her that God would punish her if she did something wrong. Maybe she never learned about God's love; how sad. Thank you, Father, for your gift of love. Help us to open up to your love."

**Have you ever met a person like Aunt Hilda?**

**Do you feel that nothing can separate you from God's love?**

# July 30

Psalm 103:8 He is merciful and tender toward those who don't deserve it; he is slow to get angry and full of kindness and love.

Sally sat hugging her bear, Muffin, next to her shoulder. She pictured Jesus standing next to her and smiling at her. "Jesus doesn't throw temper tantrums like I do. I wonder if he ever lost his temper when he was little. I can't imagine him being anything else but a very good little boy. I wish Billy would be a good little boy. My arm still hurts where he bit me yesterday. I don't know what happened. One minute, Jan and I were playing ball, and all of a sudden Billy comes up and bites me. I told Jan to keep her stupid brother away from me. So what if he is only three? He should know better. Oh, I guess I don't sound much like Jesus, either. I don't sound merciful and tender toward Billy, even if he doesn't deserve it. Jesus, please help me be like you. Help me be slow to get mad, and help me to be kind even to Billy."

**Are you able to be merciful and kind toward others?**

**Are you able to even when you feel they don't deserve it?**

# July 31

James 1:13–14 And remember, when someone wants to do wrong it is never God who is tempting him. Temptation is the pull of man's own evil thoughts and wishes.

Ted realized how close he had come to giving into temptation when he was at the Shopping Mall with Phil and Rex. "We were in the record store, and I saw a cassette tape I wanted. I checked the price, and I didn't have enough money to pay for it. The thought went through my mind that all I needed to do was to put the tape into my jacket and walk out of the store. No one would notice because the store was very busy. I even rationalized that the cassette was overpriced, so I was entitled to steal it. Wow! I said, 'steal it'! I would be shoplifting! I would be stealing! I have never stolen anything in my life. Why was I tempted to steal now? It was because I really wanted that tape, didn't have enough money, and gave into the thought of stealing the tape. Then I came to my senses. I now realize how subtle temptation can be. God, I thank you for your guidance. I realized what I was about to do was terribly wrong."

**Do you ask God to help you resist temptation?**

**Is temptation sometimes very subtle?**

# 8 August

## August 1

2 Peter 1:3 For as you know him better, he will give you, through his great power, everything you need for living a truly good life.

Amanda Adams had a great thirst for knowledge of God. "I want to learn all I can about God. I love reading scripture, and I find that each time I read, I am given new insights. Scripture is always alive and new to me. When did this thirst for the things of God come to me? When I realized that I can't depend on myself alone to live a good life. I need and I depend on God's power. I tried putting God on the back burner for a while I managed my own life without asking for his help. He watched me, giving me the freedom he gives all of us to make mistakes. I sure made my share of mistakes. I then ran back to God and asked for his help and guidance. He was there waiting for me to turn back to him. What a beautiful gift of love you give to us, God."

**Have you ever tried to manage your life without God's help?**

**Are you getting to know God better?**

## August 2

John 17:14 I have given them your commands. And the world hates them because they don't fit in with it, just as I don't.

Amy turned over in her mind the phrase "because they don't fit in with it, just as I don't." "I have never really thought about Jesus not fitting in with the world. I guess I just thought that because he was God, he would fit in anywhere. This means that Jesus really understands my hurt when the kids make fun of me because I won't go along with them and do things that I feel are wrong. They make fun of me because I go to church every Sunday and because I don't like some of the popular music groups. I don't agree with what is popular in general. I don't criticize them for what they like to do. Why then do they make fun of me? God, my biggest test is to keep my patience and to continue to feel love for them. As you said on the cross 'forgive them for they know not what they do.'"

**What are some popular things of the world that you refuse to go along with?**

**Do you fit in with ways of the world?**

# August 3

Romans 10:8 For salvation that comes from trusting Christ—which is what we preach—is already within easy reach of each of us. In fact, it is as near as our own hearts and mouths.

Jim Adams sighed to himself and thought back to when he was still in school. "That was the time in my life when I would visit God in church whenever I felt. I had some spare time. I thought I was a pretty good Christian, too, because I even attempted to make the effort to go visit God. Then a time of great questioning came into my life, and it hit me that God wasn't only in church. He was in my heart as well. He was with me constantly. I learned that I could trust him to love me and guide me through life's joys and sorrows. Going to church was a way of sharing my love for God and his love for me with others. Thank you, Lord, for being as near as my own heart and my own mouth."

**Are you able to trust God?**

**Is he as near as your own heart and your own mouth?**

# August 4

1 Chronicles 29:14 Everything we have has come from you, and we only give you what is yours already.

Jake agreed. "You know, that is very true. God has given us everything from our earth and sky, our family and friends, and our talents and gifts. Everything good comes from God. I can get pretty smug filled with my own ego when I win a wrestling match, a baseball game, or anything else that I feel was of my own making. God has really given my family and me such a good life. So when I decide to offer any of my talents to help God help others, I am only giving back talents God gave to me in the first place. God, please help me continually realize that I am nothing without you. I wouldn't even exist if you hadn't given me the gift of life. Wow! I wouldn't even be here without you. Thank you, God, for the gift of life."

**What gifts can you use to help others?**

**Other than the gift of life, what is your favorite gift from God?**

# August 5

Luke 10:16 Then he said to the disciples, "Those who welcome you are welcoming me. And those who reject you are rejecting me. And those who reject me are rejecting God who sent me."

Sara imagines Jesus talking to his disciples. "I wonder what it was like being the first disciples of Christ, listening to and looking at Jesus in person. I wonder what he really looked like. Did the early disciples have any really good idea about who Jesus was? No, they didn't. At least not until Jesus died on the Cross and then rose from the dead. No human mind could understand such a plan of God. We humans think in terms of the way the world runs, not the way God's plans run. Jesus said that any of us who reject him are in turn rejecting God who sent him. Yes, I really wish I could be one of the disciples in the scripture; but in fact, I am already one of the disciples in the here and now. I can listen to what Jesus has to say in Scripture and also in the quiet of my heart."

**Do you feel that you are a disciple in the here and now?**

**Did the disciples really have any idea who Jesus was?**

# August 6

Matthew 6:34 "So don't be anxious about tomorrow. God will take care of your tomorrow too. Live one day at a time."

Amanda Adams smiled to herself. "I pray that I will be able with your help, Lord, to help my family understand your way of living one day at a time. I grew up in a family that felt anger and guilt about the past and anxiety about the future. What a terrible way to live. There wasn't any peace in the present moment; only anger, guilt, fear, and anxiety for the past and the future. I pray that my children will have the needed trust in your help to let go of the past and the future, knowing that you will take the burdens of both into your hands. I pray that my family will learn to live one day at a time in your peace and joy. Thank you for your graces of love and trust."

**Do you stew about the past and worry about the future? If so, how does it help to stew and to worry?**

**Is this called having faith?**

# August 7

Romans 11:33 Oh, what a wonderful God we have! How great are his wisdom, knowledge, and riches. How impossible it is for us to understand his decisions and his methods.

Jim Adams nodded his head in agreement. "Yes, it is hard to understand God's decision and his methods at times. When I see the unfairness of the world, I ask God, 'Why?' Then I realize that this is all a mystery to our human minds. I do understand that God has given each of us free choice—free will. We decide whether to follow God's ways of love or to follow negative ways of not loving, which lead to sin. The choice is ours, and each choice of not following God's ways affects us in a negative, sinful way. If we choose God's loving ways, then that positive choice will affect everything around us, including us, in a positive, loving way. Yes, our God is wonderful, great, and wise. I ask you, Lord, to guide me toward making positive, loving choices."

**Can you appreciate the mystery of God?**

**In what ways have your free will choices affected those around you?**

# August 8

Romans 14:3–4 For God has accepted them to be his children. They are God's servants, not yours. They are responsible to him, not to you. Let him tell them whether they are right or wrong.

"Oh, no!" Amy thought to herself. "Oh, God, I am so sorry. I saw Julie the other day, and we had an argument about religion. I felt that I was right and that I needed to convince her that she was wrong. I needed to straighten her out, in other words. She felt the same way about me. We didn't show love to each other, and I felt an awful wave of anger rush through me. Just as I am your servant, Julie is your servant also. Julie isn't responsible to me, and I am not responsible to her. We both are responsible to you. You will guide us, won't you? The wisdom of our belief system will prove to be either right or wrong in your time and your way. You want us both to love and respect each other and not to criticize different ways we worship you."

**Are you critical of other people's ways of worship?**

**What does God say about us judging each other?**

# August 9

James 3:17 But the wisdom that comes from heaven is first of all pure and full of quiet gentleness. Then it is peace—loving and courteous. It allows discussion and is willing to yield to others; it is full of mercy and good deeds.

Jake weighed in his mind the wisdom of this verse. "The first person who pops into my mind when I think of wisdom coming from heaven in quiet gentleness is Mother Teresa. I saw a video about her work with the poor, and you could see her gentleness, her mercy, and her good deeds. She allowed discussion and was willing to yield to others, and yet is able to get her point across through words as well as actions. If we all could have the wisdom that comes from heaven, wouldn't this be a gentle world? We all choose between the wisdom from heaven or the wisdom from the world. We humans usually choose the wisdom from the world. How sad. God, I need your help in choosing the wisdom from heaven."

**Who pops into your mind as an example of having wisdom from heaven?**

**Do you choose heavenly wisdom or wisdom from the world?**

# August 10

James 4:2–3 You long for what others have, and can't afford it. And, yet, the reason you don't have what you want is that you don't ask God for it. And even when you ask you don't get it because your whole aim is wrong—you ask only what will give you pleasure.

"Oh, that's true," Amy sighed. "All of my friends went to the lake for a week, and Mom and Dad said that I couldn't go. I had to go camping with them instead. The girls went to the lake at the same time we went camping, so really I didn't have any choice. My family wanted me to be with them, and in a way, I wanted to be with them also. I also realize that a trip to the lake with my friends would have been very expensive. They go everywhere first class, and that does make it hard to afford the things they do. I didn't pray to God that I could go with them. I knew that my motives for going weren't all that great. What were my motives? They were to be a part of the in-crowd, and to have people think I come from a rich family. Oh boy, I'm not proud of my motives. God, help me to appreciate all the blessings I do have.

When you pray to God, do you receive everything you ask for?

Does God ever seem to wait to answer your prayer?

# August 11

James 4:11 Don't criticize and speak evil about each other dear brothers. If you do, you will be fighting against God's law of loving one another.

Sara admitted to herself that she had been very critical of everything since she got back from the family camping trip. "I feel irritable and bored. We never do anything exciting, like going to a movie, or going out to get a hamburger. Every day is the same. My friends are all away on vacation except for Lottie. Mom isn't very keen about my spending much time with Lottie unless she comes here, and Lottie is bored here. She has a lot of freedom and can do anything she wants. I don't want to be critical of her, but I realize she does a lot of things that get her into deep trouble. So, I ask God to be with her. God does want me to love her. He also wants me to be thankful for all the blessings I have. Maybe I will go to the library and start doing some reading while I have the chance. It is my own fault if I am bored."

**Are you critical of others? Why?**

**What events in your life make you feel restless, bored, and irritable?**

# August 12

Psalm 33:20,22 We depend upon the Lord alone to save us. Yes, Lord let your constant love surround us, for our hopes are in you alone.

Amanda needed to read this passage. "I've been so upset this summer. The children are bored with all of their activities. Jake is restless. He wants time to fly so he can be off to college in a couple of weeks. Amy is irritated that we wouldn't let her go to the lake with her friends. We wanted her to go camping with us; besides, the trip to the lake was expensive. Ted has been busy with baseball, so he has been content, thank goodness. Sara's friends are on vacation, so there is only Lottie, who gets into a lot of trouble. I only want Lottie to come over here where I can watch after the girls. I feel for the girl. Meanwhile, Sara is a handful. Sally has been enjoying the summer, so she has been good. Jim has been working overtime, and I miss him. We all do. So I need to be reminded, God, that your constant love surrounds us. As the children grow older, I do realize that our hopes are in you alone. I place my family into your hands. Give me the guidance to be a loving wife and mother."

**Do you feel God's constant love surrounds you?**

**Does being overwhelmed by events distract you from feeling God's love?**

# August 13

Ephesians 3:17 And I pray that Christ will be more and more at home in your hearts, living within you as you trust in him. May your roots go down into the soil of God's marvelous love?

Ted was having a great summer. "Gosh, it is hard to concentrate when Mom and Dad read scripture everyday after dinner. I want to get out of the house to play baseball. It's been a great season! I'm pretty distracted aren't I, God? I haven't been thinking of you very often. Why is it when things are going great, I seldom think of you, but when things are going bad, I really start praying for help? Perhaps I'd better take this time of realization to thank you for helping me have a great baseball season. I need to be open to your love in good times as well as bad. I pray that my roots will go down into the soil of your love. I trust you to help me be thankful for all of your blessings."

**When things are going great, do you pray as often as you do when things are going wrong?**

**Are you open to God's love in good times as well as bad?**

# August 14

Ezekiel 34:15–16 "I myself will be the Shepherd of my sheep, and cause them to lay in peace, the Lord God says. I will seek my lost ones, those who strayed away, and bring them safely home again. I will put splints and bandages upon their broken limbs and heal the sick."

Sally imagined Jesus standing in a field with all the sheep walking around him. "I can see Jesus smile as he picks up one of the sheep. This reminds me of the time when Fluffy was a kitten and ran out of the house when I opened the door. Mom and Dad couldn't find Fluffy, and I was so scared. I love that little cat. He was gone all night. The next morning, we found him sitting by the door. I picked him up and held him close. He was cold and shaking. I bet Jesus feels like that when we get lost. He comes looking for us so he can hold and comfort us just like he does with his sheep. Thank you, Jesus, for loving us."

**Have you ever felt like a lost sheep?**

**What happened? Did Jesus come looking for you?**

# August 15

Jeremiah 29:11–13 For I know the plans I have for you, says the Lord. They are plans for good and not for evil, to give you a future and a hope.

Jake had been feeling very restless. "I am nervous about leaving for college, and yet I can hardly wait to get out of here. I hope I chose the right major and I hope my grades will be good. This reading says that the Lord's plans for us are for good and not for evil. He wants to give us a hopeful future with what is best for us. I will turn all of these restless feelings over to God and enjoy these few days left at home. I've been pretty hard to get along with, and the family doesn't deserve my bad moods. I am beginning to feel better and more peaceful. Thank you, Lord, for this time of family prayer. I will miss this when I am at school, but I will try to read a verse or so from scripture every day."

**What are your hopes and dreams?**

**Where does God fit into your dreams?**

# August 16

Psalm 88:1–3 Oh Jehovah, God of my salvation, I have wept before you day and night. Now hear my prayers; oh, listen to my cry, for my life is full of troubles.

Amy had been feeling down the past few days. "School will soon begin, and I have had a falling out with most of my friends. I don't feel like I belong at all, and maybe I don't. My friends are beginning to go out on dates, and no one has asked me out. I don't even know if Mom and Dad would allow me to date yet; probably not. I am going to miss having Jake at school, even though we didn't see each other often. I am going to be so alone this school year. Will I be this unpopular the rest of my life? Oh, God, help me deal with my dread of the school year. Help me to realize that I am popular with you. It doesn't matter in the scheme of life if I am popular with others. Only my life in your growing love counts. In the midst of my growing, give me a peace of mind and a sense of well-being in your love."

**Have you ever wept before the Lord day and night?**

**Did God listen to your cry?**

# August 17

John 8:12 Later, in one of his talks, Jesus said to the people, "I am the Light of the world. So if you follow me, you won't be stumbling through the darkness, for living light will flood your path."

Jim Adams reflected on this reading and remembered the dark times in his life. "I have certainly stumbled in the darkness in my lifetime. There have even been times when I didn't realize I was in the darkness, let alone stumbling. All I knew was that things didn't feel quite right. I felt anxious. Things weren't going right, but I didn't know why. I would get to the point where I felt really down and would then begin to notice the darkness. I would pick up scripture and see the light. I would realize that I had indeed been stumbling in the dark. God, help me to stay open to the light of your word and your love."

**Have you ever stumbled in the darkness?**

**How did God's light come to you?**

# August 18

Matthew 28:20 "And then teach these new disciples to obey all the commands I have given you; and be sure of this—that I am with you always, even to the end of the world."

Jake turned his mind to the Easter story and to the resurrection. "Here I am getting ready to begin a new phase in my life, and I know I feel unsure of myself. Well, just imagine how the disciples must have felt. I'm certain they were very unsure of themselves. Here the resurrected Jesus is telling them to teach the new disciples to obey the commands that he had given. Wow! Talk about beginning a new phase in a person's life! But what did Jesus promise? He promised to be with them always, even to the end of the world. Doesn't Jesus also promise each of us that he will be with us even to the end of the world? Of course he does. Jesus, help me be open to your never-ending presence in my life.

**Are you open to God's never-ending presence in your life?**

**What happens to your attitude when your mind is closed to God's presence?**

# August 19

1 John 4:16 God is love, and anyone who lives in love is living with God and God is living in him. And as we live with Christ, our love grows more perfect and complete.

Amy thought back on the talk she had with her mom earlier in the day. "I know Mom has been concerned about my feeling so lonely because of all of my friends going in different directions. Mom suggested that I talk to you, God, about helping me feel your joy and your peace despite my troubles with my friends. She said that when I am fighting your inner joy and peace, I don't act very loving. In fact, she said I could be pretty hard to get along with. That hurt, but she is right. I have been angry, and negative, and a grouch. I need to turn to you and to be open to your gift of inner peace in the midst of things going right or wrong. It doesn't matter what is happening in my life. What matters is living in your love. In doing so, my love grows more perfect and complete. Your love is my joy and my peace."

**Are you living life open to God's love and peace?**

**What triggers a negative reaction in you?**

# August 20

Psalm 17:15 But as for me, my contentment is not in wealth but in seeing you and knowing all is well between us.

Sara knew what this verse meant to her. "God, when I have done something wrong, I feel terrible. Like the other day when Mom and I were at the store, I saw a game I wanted her to buy for me. She told me I couldn't have it at that time. I felt furious. I screamed at her and told her she wasn't a good mother. She never buys me anything, and she never does anything for me. The look on her face was a look of shock mixed with hurt and embarrassment. The people in the store were looking at us. I felt ashamed. I had thrown a temper tantrum much like Sally used to when she was a toddler. That game would never bring me happiness. As soon as I would get it, I would tire of it and want something else. Nothing was well between you and me and Mom and me until I remembered to tell you both how sorry I was. My joy comes in knowing all is well between you and me and others.

**Where does your contentment come from?**

**Is all well between you and God, and you and others?**

# August 21

Revelation 3:20 "Look! I have been standing at the door and I am constantly knocking. If anyone hears me calling him and opens the door, I will come in and fellowship with him and he with me."

Jake's eyes surprised him with tears. "Why are my eyes tearing up? I leave for college tomorrow morning. This will be the last evening here with the family until Thanksgiving break. Who will I eat with in the meantime? Strangers who will become friends. What kind of friends? I don't know. Jesus is my truest friend, isn't he? He is constantly knocking at my door, and I rarely open it when I'm involved with the things of the world. When I become involved with my classes, tests, new friends, and my social life, I might really not hear Jesus knocking at my door at all. God, help me remember that you are always at my door knocking. All I have to do is open the door and let you in. Then you will fellowship with me and be my friend. You will share my classes, friends, meals, and life with me."

**Can you hear the Lord knocking at your door?**

**Are you ready to let him share your life with you?**

# August 22

Psalm 68:5 He is a Father to the Fatherless; he gives justice to the widows, for he is holy. He gives families to the lonely.

Amanda Adams's voice cracked when she read this verse. "Oh, Jake, I pray that your trip to school went well today. How we miss you, and you only left this morning. God, I know that you will look after Jake. You love him far more than we, his human family, are able to love anyone. You are a father to us and a father to Jake. You will find a family of people to be there for Jake when he needs friends. When he feels lonely, I pray that you will help me release Jake's welfare into your hands. I ask that you will help me continually realize that you are watching over Jake. I, as his mother, cannot protect him from harm as I did when he was a baby. Please give me your peace of mind, and help me feel joy in my aching heart."

**Have you ever been away from familiar surroundings and felt lonely?**

**What helped you adjust to your new surroundings?**

# August 23

Psalm 69-:32 The humble shall see their God work for them. No wonder they will be so glad! All who seek for God shall live in joy.

Jim Adams was relieved when Jake called and said he had a good trip and was settled in at the dorm. He had a great roommate, so all was well. "Thank you, God, for looking after Jake. I am glad he is settled in at his dorm and has a good roommate. I pray that Jake will continue to realize how you are at work in his life. The humility that comes from the realization that none of us can do anything well without your help is the foundation of the freedom a joyful heart experiences. What joy and what freedom comes to us when we know you are behind us loving and helping. At times we may not feel that you are helping or even loving us, but if we have a strong foundation of faithful humility, we will feel joy in our hearts even in the midst of trials. Thank you, Lord. I know you will take good care of Jake. We all love him so much."

**What does humility mean to you?**

**Are you able to put your trust in the wisdom of the Lord?**

# August 24

Jeremiah 29:12–13 In those days when you pray, I will listen. You will find me when you seek me, if you look for me in earnest.

"This is true God," agreed Amy. "When I seek you I do find you. But so often I get caught up in my problems and you seen so far away. In the scheme of things, my problems are so petty. I feel like you wouldn't possibly be interested. I don't feel you would listen, so I don't even think of you. I don't think of you until I become so miserable that I come to you as a last resort. Then you help me, and things go fine for a while, and then the whole cycle starts again when new problems crop up. Mom says that we should be aware of your presence at all times, in good times and bad time. I need to establish an on going relationship with you, God. I need to look for you in earnest at all times, don't I? Please give me your spirit to help me be aware of your love and presence at all times."

**At what times do you seek God?**

**Do you have an on-going relationship with God?**

# August 25

1 Corinthians 4:7 What are you so puffed up about? What do you have that God hasn't given you? And if all you have is from God, why act as though you are so great, as though you have accomplished something on your own?

"Well, that sure does put me in my place," laughed Ted to himself. "I really acted like a jerk after winning the baseball championship game the other day. I really felt like I had won it on my own. Needless to say, a couple of my buddies brought me back to earth by saying I had the team to thank also. Without their help, I couldn't have pitched the winning game. And now I have St. Paul telling me the same thing. Yes, all I have has come from God, talents and all. So if all is from God, why am I acting like I am so great? It's funny how these feelings of pride come over me. They are so subtle. They sneak up on me and before I know it, I am acting like a jerk. God, please give me a good sense of self-esteem based on knowing you are the one who is great. Thank you."

**Have you ever been puffed up, taking all the credit for your talents?**

**What happened?**

# August 26

2 Corinthians 6:3 We try to live in such a way that no one will ever be offended or kept back from finding the Lord by the way we act, so that no one can find fault with us and blame it on the Lord.

Sara met some of her friends at the park for a picnic, and she had felt bothered ever since. "God, we made fun of Lori because she didn't want to leave the park and go on over to the shopping mall without getting permission from her mother first. We called her a baby, and we left her sitting on the picnic bench with a mess of paper plates and stuff to clean up. We just walked away from her. If she didn't want to go with us, we would just leave her with the mess. Well, Lori was planning on coming to our church in September, and now I don't know if she will even want to. We were in the wrong because we should have asked our moms if we could go to the Mall, also. In fact I'd better tell Mom the truth about going to the Mall without her permission. She thinks we were at the park all afternoon. I'd better call Lori and apologize. I apologize to you too, God. I'm so sorry."

**Have you ever made a bad impression on someone who knew you were a follower of Christ?**

**What did you do to correct the situation?**

# August 27

Philippians 2:3–4 Don't be selfish; don't live to make a good impression on others. Don't just think about your own affairs, but be interested in others, too, and in what they are doing.

"Oh, God, that's what I want to do," sighed Amy. "I don't want to be selfish. I don't want to be with my friends and worry about how I must be coming across to them. I even go so far as to becoming angry if their reaction to me is less than friendly. The other day, Nancy didn't pay any attention to what I was saying. I felt so mad at her. I later found out that Nancy's mother was in the hospital for major surgery and Nancy was worried. Nancy was not about to concentrate on what I was saying. I must call Nancy to see how her mother is doing. Also, I want to see how Nancy is feeling. I really need to have your help, God, in showing interest in others and not always just thinking about my own affairs. I need your help, God, because I am just too weak to be compassionate towards others on my own."

**When you are with people, do you worry about what kind of and impression you are making on others?**

**What kind of help do you need from God in showing interest in others?**

# August 28

James 3:17 But wisdom that comes from heaven is first of all pure and full of quiet gentleness. Then it is peace loving and courteous. It allows discussion and is willing to yield to others.

"Allowing discussion and being willing to yield to others is a very hard thing for me to do," brooded Amanda Adams. "The other evening at our monthly women's group meeting, June once again got on her negative platform and hogged the whole meeting. She is such a difficult person. June is certainly not quiet and gentle, let alone peace loving and courteous. But then neither am I when it comes to dealing with June. I leave the meetings feeling frustrated and very angry. There must be some way of allowing June to have her say, and yet allow the other women to voice their concerns and views also. God, please guide our group. Please help June, and help me in dealing with June in a peace-loving and courteous way. Perhaps I will go to the library and check out some books on the subject of dealing with difficult people. I will continue to pray for your guidance, God."

**Do you have a gentle spirit filled with God's wisdom?**

**How do you handle difficult people?**

# August 29

1 Timothy 2:1–2 I urge, then, first of all, that requests, prayers, intercession and thanksgiving be made for everyone—for kings and all those in authority, that we may live peaceful and quiet lives in all godliness and holiness.

"God, why did I have to get Mrs. Spencer for chemistry?" cried Amy. "She is the meanest, hardest teacher in the whole high school.

What a rotten first day of school this has been. I miss Jake so much. I could use his help with chemistry. He had Mrs. Spencer and finally ended up with some pretty good grades. Of course Jake is smart. Well, I will pray for Mrs. Spencer. I will ask God to help her teach us. I will pray for her as well as the rest of my teachers so they will have the gifts given by God to teach us. And I will pray that I will have an open mind to receive the education these teachers are working so hard to pass on to us. I wish Mrs. Spencer my best. Help me to like her and to understand her. Thank you, God, for all you are going to do."

**Has there ever been a time when you had a teacher you had difficulty with?**

**Did you ask God for help, and did you pray for that teacher?**

# August 30

Luke 12:25–26 "And besides, what's the use of worrying? What good does it do? Will it add a single day to your life? Of course not! And if worry can't even do such little things as that, what's the use of worrying over bigger things?"

Jim Adams often remembered this scripture reading when he found himself concerned about finances. "I needed to be reminded that worrying doesn't help matters. Worrying drains energy and causes sleepless nights. With Jake off to college and Amy being a junior in high school with college around the corner, I wonder where the extra money will come from. Tuition has really risen. Then both Ted and Sara need to wear braces, so the Orthodontist's bill is going to be great. I must put my trust in you, God, I know. Jake has a good job lined up for working this coming summer. Amy plans on working also next summer. That will help. Summer jobs have been hard to come by, so we are blessed to have these two jobs lined up starting next June. You are answering my prayer, God."

**Are you able to turn your worries over to God?**

**What happened when you put your trust in God?**

# August 31

1 Timothy 6:6 Do you want to be truly rich? You already are if you are happy and good.

Sally thought about this verse and about the meaning being rich. "On TV I've seen people say that being rich is having lots of money. They say that if you have lots of money, you can buy all the toys you want, and that will make you happy. Then I've heard Mom and Dad say that money can't buy happiness. That gets confusing to me. What this verse is saying then is that being rich doesn't mean having lots of money. It means that if you are happy and good, then you are already rich. I don't know about how good I am, but I think that for the most part I am good. I do know that I am very happy, though. I had a lot of fun this summer. And then school starts in a few days, and I will be in the first grade. I'm looking forward to that. You know what; I am very rich, aren't I?"

**Are you happy and good?**

**Do you feel God's peace and joy?**

# September

## September 1

2 Corinthians 10:17 As the Scriptures say, "If anyone is going to boast, let him boast about what the Lord has done and not about himself. "

Ted laughed to himself. "I wish Jeff could hear this verse. I've never met a guy who thought so much of himself. I must admit that he is a great baseball player. He is good at football and will probably make junior varsity this year. He makes good grades, also. He is always bragging about how great he is. This turns people off, and they don't want to be around him. He always can top anything that is said. Who wants to compete in just everyday conversation? Who needs it? Yeah, what a difference it would make in Jeff's life if he were only able to think about all the things the Lord has done, not only for the world, but for him as well. That would put a stop to Jeff's bragging. I will keep Jeff in my prayers, God. Amen."

**Do you ever find yourself boasting?**

**What can you tell others about the Lord has done rather than focusing on yourself?**

## September 2

Philippians 4::12 I know how to live on almost nothing or with everything. I have learned the secret of contentment in every situation whether it be full stomach or hunger, plenty or want.

Amanda Adams nodded her head in agreement. "Yes, with God's help of strength and courage, we can learn the secret of contentment in every situation. I guess this would be called God's peace and joy, which is found within one's heart. God's joy isn't dependent on outside forces. It is a stable force coming from within us. I pray that I will also be able to live on almost nothing and also with everything. What freedom such an attitude is. And what is the secret of contentment in every situation? The secret is that I do everything God asks me to because Christ gives me the power and the strength to do so. Verse twelve says just that. Now all I have to do is to remember this not only with my mind but with my heart. I ask you, God, in the name of Jesus, to bring this message to my heart. Amen."

**Do you want to know how to live in contentment both in times of want and times of plenty?**

**How can God help you?**

# September 3

Psalm 27:14 Don't be impatient. Wait for the Lord, and he will come and save you! Be brave, and stouthearted and courageous. Yes, wait and he will help you.

"Oh God," sighed Amy. "School begins tomorrow, and I am so nervous. On one hand I'm impatient to begin so I can get into a new routine. On the other hand, I dread all the new situations that will be coming up. It would help if I had a good friend but, I don't. My heart aches for a good friend. All the people I know are so shallow. Mom and Dad keep saying that you are my good friend, Jesus, but you seem so far away. I don't think you would be very interested in teenage girl talk, either. But then maybe you would after all. You do care about what happens to each of us. You don't get bored with us like our friends do. You are faithful to us no matter what. Yes, Lord, I know you will help me, so I will enjoy this evening. "

**In what ways has the Lord come to save you?**

**Is it hard to remember to turn to the Lord?**

# September 4

James 5:9 Don't grumble about each other, brothers. Are you, yourselves, above criticism?

Amy was in tears. "God, I hoped you would be with me when I went to school. Where were you? I felt so alone. I had a mix-up with which homeroom I was to be in. Then my locker wouldn't open. At lunch I couldn't find a table because I was late and ended up sitting with some stupid ninth graders. I ran late all day. By the time I got to each of my classes, I had to sit in seats no one else wanted. I waited for some of the people I know to come up to me to say hello. They knew I was having troubles with my schedule. Did they help? No, they didn't." Amy paused. "Would I have helped someone today? No. In fact, the other people were having problems, too. I didn't even think about them. The whole school was in an uproar because of computer errors in the scheduling. God, you were with me. The day ended up okay. I got to my classes and I got my locker opened. Thank you, God."

**Do you ever grumble about others?**

**Are you above others?**

# September 5

Mark 9:50 "Good salt is worthless if it loses its saltiness, it can't season anything. So don't lose your flavor! Live in peace with each other."

Jim Adams immediately thought about his boss. "I don't know what has happened to Ken. He used to be a fair-minded guy who always gave people lots of encouragement. I never know what to expect out of Ken now. He is patient one minute, and the next minute he will become irritated and make sarcastic remarks. He isn't like himself at all. I guess I could say that Ken has lost his saltiness. Morale is down, and we tread lightly around him. In fact, his work has been going downhill. Lots of reports are late, and we carefully remind him that he needs to look over the reports we prepared and sign them. I wonder if something is wrong in his life. I put Ken into your care, God. Help me keep my patience with Ken and be there for him if he needs me. Amen."

**Do you know anyone who has lost his flavor?**

**Are you able to live in peace with others?**

# September 6

Psalm 107:1 Say "Thank you" to the Lord for being so good, for always being so loving and kind. Has the Lord redeemed you? Then speak out!

Amy shouted in her heart with joy. "God, I love school! You have been right there beside me. Thank you for my new friend, Linda. I met her yesterday in history class, and we took a liking to each other. She just moved here before school began, so she needs help in finding her way around school. As I was showing her where her next class was, we found that we really had a lot in common.

We even ate lunch together. Linda came over here after school. We studied together and talked mostly girl talk. You were there, Jesus, listening and sharing our lives with us.

To think I was feeling blue just a few days ago, and now I feel so happy. I love school. I have Linda for a friend, and most of all, Lord, I have your love, kindness, and friendship. Thank you. Amen."

**When have you shouted for joy because of God's love and kindness?**

**Did you tell others about God's love?**

# September 7

1 Timothy 6:11 Oh, Timothy, you are God's man. Run from all these evil things and work instead at what is right and good, learning to trust him and love others, and to be patient and gentle.

Ted felt worn out. "Man, am I tired. Football practice was fierce, and it looks like I am not going to make the team. It's probably just as well because I am really going to have to hit the books this year. Plus, I would like to build up my lawn care business. I let things slide this summer due to baseball, but I need some spending money. Without playing football, I can work and earn some extra cash and save some money for college. I guess I am also asked to work at what is right and good. I will trust God and be patient and gentle to others. God, I sure need your help in loving others and being patient, let alone gentle. I do trust you to help me and guide me in working for what is right and good. I need to study. I need to save some money for college, and I need to know you better, God. Thank you for your guidance. Amen."

**Do you work for what is right and good?**

**How does God help you?**

# September 8

Psalm 131:1–3 Lord, I am not proud and haughty. I don't think myself better than others. I don't pretend to know it all. I am quiet now before the Lord.

Sara had a hard time at religion class. "I really am quiet before the Lord now. I went to religion class today, and Mrs. Lewis really embarrassed me. We were talking about scripture, and I knew just about all of the answers, so I kept interrupting others before they could give their answers. I really did think I was better than them because I felt I knew more about God. I felt a false pride, and I was belittling others. Mrs. Lewis finally told me, in a gentle way, to allow the others in our class to answer some questions. I felt so embarrassed and also sad. Just once I felt I knew some answers, and I'm asked to be quiet? Well, actually, I didn't really know all the answers. I was just pretending to. I'm sorry, God, that I acted like I did. Help me to be thoughtful towards others. Amen."

**Have you ever been proud and haughty?**

**What happened?**

# September 9

Psalm 81:6–7 I heard an unknown voice that said, "Now I will relieve your shoulder of its burden; I will free your hands from its heavy tasks." He said "You cried to me in trouble and I saved you."

Amanda Adams had felt blue the past few days. "I don't know what is wrong with me. I guess my life is at another point of change. Jake is away at college, Amy is in the 11th grade, Ted is in the 9th grade, Sara is in the 7th grade, and my baby, Sally, is in the 1st grade. My children are growing up, and so life changes for them as well as for Jim and me. So often, God, over the years, I have heard an inner insight from you saying that you would relieve my shoulder of its burden. I am okay for a while, then I take on a new burden to shoulder. I just don't automatically turn my burdens over to you, do I? You always hear my cry when the burden becomes too much for me to carry. I need to learn that releasing my cares to you in the first place would bring me the joy and peace I yearn for. Help me trust you, God. Amen."

**Do you release your cares and worries into the Lord's hands?**

**When you cry for help, does God hear you?**

# September 10

Timothy 2:4–5 For he longs for all to be saved and to understand this truth: That God is on one side and all the people on the other side, and Christ Jesus, he is between to bring them together, by giving his life for all mankind.

Amy mulled this over in her mind. "I can picture God standing on the bank of a river and waving at all of us people standing on the other side. God is trying to get our attention to tell us that he loves us, but we are too busy fighting with each other. Once in a while, someone might notice God over there and point him out to us. We may even wave back, but before long we are fighting each other again. Then up walks a man. Many of us notice him. We want to listen to him speak, but we don't understand what he is saying. We think he is going to stop our fighting and become our king. He makes some people very angry. They kill him. That man is Jesus. He rises from the dead and builds a bridge over the river so we can cross over to visit God. It is up to us if we want to follow Jesus or not."

**Are you waving back to God on the other shore?**

**Are you crossing the bridge with Jesus and walking towards God?**

# September 11

Psalm 101-2 I will try to walk a blameless path, but how I need your help, especially in my own home, where I long to act as I should.

Ted felt embarrassed. "I wonder if Mom read this verse to give me a message loud and clear. Well, no matter—this verse applies to me. I do need your help, God. I have really been hard to get along with. Not making the football team really made me angry, and I have been taking my anger and frustration out on everyone around me.

I've yelled at Sally, teased Sara, ignored Amy, and refused to do anything that Mom and Dad requested me to do. I even refused to talk to anyone at the dinner table. I feel like a failure, so I am striking out at people as though it is their fault. I need to examine myself to set new goals and to stop measuring my worth through outside events. I know from deep inside me that I am very worthwhile person. You, God, have made each of us worthwhile. Thank you."

**Do you ever take your frustrations out on other people, particularly family members?**

**If so, do you ask for God's help?**

# September 12

Exodus 4:10 But Moses pleaded, "Oh Lord, I'm just not a good speaker. I never have been, and I'm not now, even after you have spoken to me, for I have a speech impediment."

Sally interrupted the quiet time with a question. "Mom, what does that long word mean? Moses had problem?" Her Mother nodded yes. Sally tried to figure what kind of a problem Moses had "I wonder if he couldn't speak loud enough. That is what my teacher, Mrs. Well's, says about me. She is constantly asking me to speak louder. I hate to raise my hand and answer a question now because I feel self-conscious about my quiet voice. If God had asked me to speak to a crowd, I would have to refuse like Moses. I would have to say no. but then if I remember right, Moses was a Jewish leader. He had something to do with the Ten Commandments. I guess God helped Moses with his speech problem. God, will you help me to talk louder? Thank you, God.

**Do you find it hard to express yourself well under certain conditions?**

**How can god give you the courage to speak up?**

# September 13

Jeremiah 31:33 But this is the new contract I will make with them: I will inscribe my laws upon their hearts so that they shall want to honor me; then they shall truly be my people and I will be their God.

Amanda Adams's eyes teared up as Jim read this verse. "How beautiful. The Jewish people lived by these laws. They obeyed them to the letter. The laws became their God and their idol. In the process, they actually forgot about God, who is love. Jesus came and told the people that he hadn't come to abolish the laws and the warnings of the prophets. He said he had come to fulfill them, and every law would continue until its purpose was achieved. The new contract was that Jesus brought the gift of God's love that helped these laws into our hearts. When we love as God loves, we automatically want to obey the laws and be God's people. We do this because we truly love God. We no longer keep the laws because someone else tells us we should. We keep the laws because we want to."

**Do you keep God's laws because someone tells you to?**

**Or do you keep the laws because they are in your heart?**

# September 14

John 15:9–10 "I have loved you even as the Father has loved me. Live within my love. When you obey me, you are living in my love, just as I obey my Father and live in his love.

Ted wondered, "What does Jesus mean? What exactly does Jesus ask us to do? What does he want us to obey? Well, he said he wanted us to love God, his Father, with our whole hearts, minds and souls. Jesus then asks us to love each other as we love ourselves. He asks us to live in his love, just as he lives in his Father's love. He obeys his Father and loves him. He asks us to live in his love, to obey him and to love him. The one thing I find hard to do is love myself! I get pretty down on myself at times. Then I find it hard to love God and to love people. I feel so angry about myself. But then I must remember that God loves me unconditionally. He asks me to at least give myself respect and compassion, and to do the same for others,"

**Are you able to give yourself love, respect, and compassion?**

**Are you able to forgive yourself?**

# September 15

Philippians 4: 8 Fix your thoughts on what is true and good and right. Think about things that are pure and lovely and dwell on the fine, good things in others.

Jim Adams thought back on his phone conversation with Jake. "If Jake would ever ask me for advice, I would quote this verse to him. What a verse of wisdom this is for all of us. At this point in time, Jake appears to be trying to do what is true, good, and right. He is enjoying college and seems to be doing well in most of his classes. With the exception of one of his college friends, Nick, he enjoys their company, and this one troublesome friend has brought out a caring side of Jake. He is truly trying to see the good in the guy despite the fact that Nick is on his case all the time. I am really proud of Jake. God, you are working in Jake. Thank you

**Are you able to dwell on the fine, good things in others?**

**Do you think about things that are pure and lovely?**

# September 16

2 Timothy 2:16–17 Steer clear of foolish discussions, which lead people into the sin of anger with each other. Things will be said that will burn and hurt for a long time.

Amanda Adams had attended a church meeting that left her feeling down. "I don't feel very good about myself this morning. It seemed like every topic that came up last night I felt anger toward; however, I feel that people have a right to their opinions. We are all different. I like these people so much, and I want to get along with them. I respect their views. I finally spoke up with my point of view, and someone ridiculed my view and said it didn't apply to the situation at all. He asked me where I had been all evening. Had I been listening, or had I been daydreaming? I was stunned speechless. Everyone laughed and went on with the discussion. God, please heal the hurt I am feeling. The discussion last night wasn't foolish, but the put downs were.

**When have foolish discussions led you to anger?**

**How did you handle anger?**

# September 17

2 Corinthians 12:9 Each time he said, 'No. But I am with you; that is all you need. My power shows up best in weak people." Now I am glad to boast about how weak I am.

Amy's eyes filled with tears. "I wish I had some talents. I am weak in just about everything. I don't sing. I don't play sports very well. I don't play a musical instrument. My grades are okay, but I have to work very hard for the grades I get. School doesn't come easily to me. I don't know what I am going to major in when I go to college. Maybe it will be teaching. I can feel real empathy for those students who are weak in their studies. I think I would make a good teacher, except I find it hard to get up and talk in front of others because I am so shy. God, how can you work through all of my weaknesses? Maybe it is because if a person is weak, he needs your help. He also is able feel empathy towards others."

**In what areas are you weak?**

**How can God work through these weaknesses?**

# September 18

Hebrews 4:15 This High Priest of ours understands our weakness, since he had the same temptation we do, though he never once gave way to them and sinned.

Ted liked this reading very much. "To think that Jesus understands our weaknesses means a lot to me .When I lose my temper, I know that Jesus understands this emotion. However, he never gave in to the temptation of going around angry by feeling resentment. Jesus knew how to express his anger in a positive way. I express my anger in a negative way and end up hurting others and myself, as well. Jesus didn't allow his emotions to control him. I ask you, Jesus, for to help me control my emotions instead of my emotions controlling me. Amen"

**Do your emotions control you, or do you control them?**

**Does it bring comfort to you in knowing that Jesus understands you?**

# September 19

Psalm 37:23 The steps of good men are directed by the Lord. He delights in each step they take. If they fail it isn't fatal, for the Lord holds them with his hand.

Sara found these words to be comforting. "So many times I do things that I know I shouldn't. The other day I was sitting in the school cafeteria eating lunch. I'm afraid I was joining in with the kids at my table when they cut down the kids at other tables. We even laughed at them. It made all of us feel smug, like we were better than them. Then a new girl asked if she could sit at our table because all of the other tables were taken. We continued making fun of different ones in the cafeteria. I looked at the new girl, and I saw tears in her eyes. I felt awful. I asked her what her name was and she said it was Paula. I realized how awful we looked in the eyes of Paula, and also in the eyes if God. Forgive me."

**Have you ever cut others down?**

**How did you feel?**

# September 20

Psalm 119:1 Happy are all who perfectly follow the laws of God. Happy are all who search for God, and always do his will.

Sally was heartbroken this evening. Mrs. Stone, her first grade teacher, had called her mother because Sally had cheated in class that morning. "I wasn't cheating, though. I know my eyes fell on Suzanne's paper. I was wondering if Suzanne was almost done. I knew the answers, but I looked like I was cheating. The rule was to keep your eyes on your own paper. God, I want to do what you want me to, even if that means keeping my eyes on my own paper. I feel so ashamed. I thank you, God, for Mom's love and hug. Suzanne and I jumped rope together on the playground. She is so nice. Please guide me God.

**Are you searching for God's guidance?**

**Have you ever been tempted to cheat?**

# September 21

Romans 13:9 If you love your neighbor as much as you love yourself you will not want to harm or cheat him, or kill him or steal from him.

Sara was fed up. "I get so tired of Harry teasing Paula and me. Why does he have to keep making trouble for everyone? I guess he doesn't love his neighbor as much as he loves himself. Maybe he doesn't love himself very much, either. I never thought about that before. Maybe he is trying to get attention, and the only way he knows how to get attention is to tease and bully everyone around him. God, I pray that Harry will come to realize that his need for attention is coming across in a very hurtful way to himself and others. In the meantime, help me be patient with him. Help me to ignore his teasing. If I ignore him, I won't be giving him the attention he wants."

**Do you love your neighbor as much as you love yourself?**

**When you love a person, don't you want to give them respect?**

# September 22

1 Peter 3: 9 Don't repay evil for evil. Don't snap at those who say unkind things about you. Instead, pray for God's help for them, for we are to be kind to others.

"I really blew it today," Ted thought to himself, "Why didn't I just let it go? Sure, Jeff is an arrogant guy. Everyone knows that. Why couldn't I just ignore him? No, I go and give him a punch on the chin. He, of course, gives me a good wallop. Then we were punching each other with guys cheering us on. Well, Jeff isn't only arrogant; he is a good fighter as well. I got a black eye and bruised pride. Mom and Dad weren't very happy with me, either. I was stupid to react to Jeff's remarks like I did. God, what I need to do is pray to you to help Jeff. Please help me overcome my negative feelings about Jeff."

**Have you ever repaid evil with evil?**

**What were the results?**

# September 23

Philippians 2:3–4 Don't be selfish; don't live to make a good impression on others. Don't just think about your own affairs, but be interested in others, too, and in what they are doing.

"That is just about what Linda said to me today." Amy sighed. "I was trying to make a good impression on the group of students who were visiting our school. Linda and I had been asked to show them around, and I just about turned cartwheels trying to impress them. I don't know what got into me. I wouldn't allow Linda to talk at all. I was only interested in myself and their reaction to me. I was selfish, and I must call Linda to tell her that I am sorry. I want to apologize to you, God.

**Do you try to make a good impression on others?**

**Have you ever wanted to make a good impression on others?**

# September 24

Ephesians 5:1–2, Follow God's example in everything you do just as a much loved child imitates his father. Be full of love for others, following the example of Christ who loved you.

Jim Adams thought about coming to God as a little child. "Yes, a child does try to imitate his parents and his family. A child is trusting and so innocent. Then comes the time when an older child might begin to think that he knows best. That's when the rebellion begins. He stops looking up to his parents, feeling they don't know anything.

Also, he feels that God doesn't know anything either. I then began to realize that my parents were pretty smart after all. God really did know what he was talking about. Thank you, God, for your guidance to come to my senses

**Did you ever rebel against authority?**

**Why is it so hard for us humans to find peace?**

# September 25

Ephesians 6:4 And now a word to you parents. Don't keep on scolding and nagging your children, making them angry and resentful. Rather, bring them up with the loving discipline the Lord himself approves with suggestions and Godly advice.

Amanda Adams' brother, Jerry, was arriving the next day for a three-day visit. "I always dread Jerry's visits. I love him and I care about him, but I do not like the way he criticizes Jim and the children. He criticizes everything I do, also. None of us can do anything right in his eyes. Because I love Jerry, I have always ignored his put-downs. Starting tomorrow, I am going to tell Jerry that I don't need correction, free advice, or put-downs. I know Jerry will become very angry and will stir up my mom and dad, but I will not allow Jerry to treat my husband, my children, or me in this fashion any longer. God, please help me use my anger at Jerry in a constructive way. Nagging and scolding not only make children angry and resentful, but adults react in the same way."

**Have you ever been around a person who points out everything he feels you are doing wrong?**

**What is your reaction? Do you turn to God for help?**

# September 26

John 9:39 Then Jesus told him, "I have come into the world to give sight to those who are spiritually blind and to show those who think they see that they are blind."

Jim Adams laughed to himself. "Jerry has only been in the house one hour. Already he has told me I needed to put lime on my yard, paint my front door, reseal my driveway, and put a new roof on the house. Poor Amanda fixed this wonderful dinner, and Jerry didn't like anything she fixed. He hasn't started on the kids yet. God, here Jerry sits across the table from me. I ask you to give him sight to see how he hurts people with his negative comments. I really believe that he thinks he is showing concern, yet there is a part of me that questions his motives. God, guide us and give us the freedom from the negative, angry reactions we all feel. Give us wisdom. Give us your compassion so that we can love and accept Jerry as he is, yet not allow him to invade our lives. Amen."

**When have you been spiritually blind?**

**What happened?**

# September 27

Colossians 3:21 Fathers, don't scold your children so much that they become discouraged and quit trying.

Ted wondered if this verse applied to uncles, also. "What's with Uncle Jerry? He wondered why I didn't make the football team. He assumed it was because I wasn't eating right, so he gave me a lecture on what foods I needed to eat. He asked me what my grades were. I made the mistake of telling him, so another lecture came. He felt that my mom and dad weren't strict enough with me. Then he lectured Sara on the importance of being outgoing. Uncle Jerry felt she was too shy. On and on he went. The only one he didn't criticize was Amy because she stayed out of his way. Little Sally cried when Uncle Jerry told her that her printing was terrible. God, how can we respond to Uncle Jerry when he treats us with his negative thoughts about us? How can we express ourselves and yet be respectful to him?"

**How do you react to someone's unfair criticisms of you?**

**What is the difference between fair, constructive criticism and unfair criticism?**

# September 28

Matthew 23:11–12 "The more lowly you service to others, the greater you are. To be the greatest, be a servant. But those who think themselves great shall be disappointed and humbled, and those who humble themselves shall be exalted."

Amanda Adams felt such sadness. "Jerry left today extremely angry with me. I told him in a very calm way that I did not want him to point out any more flaws he saw in my family, my house, or my dog and cat. I did not want to hear anymore about what he felt was good or bad for us. I told him that he was not an expert on anything pertaining to my life or my family. So be it, God. The situation is in your hands. I know my mom and dad will be angry at Jim and me because they can't see any flaws in Jerry. I pray that

Jerry will know that we all love him very much. We have put our boundaries in place, and we cannot allow him to cross over those boundary lines. Please give Jerry your peace and joy. Thank you for your wisdom, Father. Amen."

**Have you ever had to tell someone that he was crossing your boundary lines?**

**What happened?**

# September 29

1 Peter 1:2 And the Holy Spirit has been at work in your hearts, cleansing you with the blood of Jesus Christ and making you please him. May God bless you richly and grant you increasing freedom from all anxiety and fear.

Jim Adams felt like breathing a sigh of relief. "Thank you, God, for answering our prayers. Jerry called Amanda today and gave her an apology. He said he was sorry that he acted like he was an expert about our family. He said he was glad she told him how she felt. Now he can change his behavior because she let him know she was upset. Later, Amanda's mom called to tell her how happy she was that Jerry had such a nice visit with us. I wished we would have told Jerry sooner, but we didn't want to cause trouble. I now feel that we can be free from all anxiety we have when Jerry visits. The Holy Spirit has been in our hearts, showing us how to set limits in a positive way."

**Do you know how to set limits in a positive way?**

**Do you feel free from fear and anxiety?**

# September 30

1 Peter 2: 22–23 Follow in his steps; He never sinned, never told a lie, never answered back when insulted; when he suffered he did not threaten to get even; he left his case in the hands of God who always judges fairly.

"Wow,," Ted exclaimed to himself! "Those are hard steps to follow. I have such a hot temper that I don't know if I will ever be able to leave a situation in God's hands to take care of it. Before I know it, when I get angry, I want to strike out. I want revenge. I want to get even. I wonder why I act like that. What is at stake? I guess it is my self-esteem. I feel like I am being attacked, so I need to stand up for myself. Is that actually a sign of me having low self-esteem? I bet it is. If I had high self-esteem, it wouldn't really matter to me if someone insulting me or not. I bet I wouldn't have such a hot temper if my self-esteem were high. Do I accept myself as I am, with all my faults and flaws? I guess I don't. God, help me get to know myself and accept what I find. Amen."

**Do you ever lose your temper?**

**Do you have a sense of good self-esteem?**

# 10 October

## October 1

Romans 14:12–13 Yes, each of us will give an account of himself to God. So don't criticize each other anymore.

Amy knew this was a verse she needed to take seriously. "Why am I so critical of everyone at school? I guess I am angry at them because I don't feel like they like me. I guess I really am the main person who doesn't like me. I want to be pretty, smart and popular. I am really just plain average, and I don't stand out in a group. I want to get some attention, but instead I just get ignored. I am very quiet, so people don't notice that I am around. That makes me mad, and then I don't feel very good about myself. My self-esteem drops, and then I strike out by criticizing everyone. This is to try to make myself look better than others. Of course all it does is to make me a person who other people don't want to be around because of all of my criticism. God, please heal me of my low self-esteem. Help me to love myself so that I can love others.

**Do you criticize and judge others?**

**Why?**

# October 2

Galatians 5:15 But if instead of showing love among yourselves you are always critical and catty, watch out! Beware of ruining each other.

"Oh boy," Sara sighed. "I feel so bad. I have been feeling very angry at Jody. She can be so sarcastic and snotty to me. She doesn't like me at all, and she doesn't hide her feelings. So why did I strike out in a sarcastic way at Jody today? Why was I so catty? That wasn't nice of me. I really didn't even know that I had hurt Jody until Paula whispered to me that Jody left the room in tears. I felt awful. I did to Jody what I have felt she has done to me. Two wrongs don't make a right. Just because Jody treats me in a sarcastic, critical way is no excuse to treat her the same. All I needed to say is that I don't want her to speak to me like that again. But now I can't because I have done the same thing to her. God, please give me the wisdom I need in handling difficult people. Help me to be loving and compassionate. Amen."

**How do you handle difficult people?**

**Do you strike out, or do you tell them in a gentle way that you don't like their behavior towards you?**

# October 3

Ephesians 4:29 Say only what is good and helpful to those you are talking to and what will give them a blessing.

Amy liked what this verse was saying. "It is true. When we say only what is good and helpful to others, it is giving them a blessing. The other day, Mom took me aside and gently told me that I was using too much make-up on my face. I was angry with her at first, but when I looked at myself in the mirror, I really did have an awful lot of make-up on my face. I washed it all off and applied new make-up very lightly. I guess I had gotten so used to seeing my make-up, I was putting more and more on, thinking it would show up better. Later, I thanked Mom for telling me. I realize that along with giving people encouragement, building them up and making them feel good about themselves, there is also helpful criticism given in a gentle way like Mom did for me."

**Do you only say what is good and helpful to others?**

**Have you ever torn anyone down? What happened, and how did you feel?**

# October 4

2 Colossians 2:6 And now just as you trusted Christ to save you, trust him, too, for each day's problems; live in vital union with him.

Jim Adams remembered back when he felt that God was very far away. "Yes, indeed, God did seem distant to me. The only place I thought I could talk to him was kneeling at the side of my bed each night. I asked God to watch over us during the night. I said grace before meals. We also went to church each Sunday. God didn't seem to be around any other time. Since God was so distant, I tried to take care of my own problems with my own limited human wisdom, and that could certainly be a disaster at times. I was relieved when I learned that God is with us at all times. I can freely turn to him and ask for his help with my daily problems, trusting him to help me in his way and time. I thank you, God, for loving me and for listening to me. Help me quiet down so that I will listen to what you have to say to me."

**Do you believe that God is with your at all times?**

**Do you trust God with each day's problems?**

# October 5

James 1:19–20 Dear brothers, don't ever forget that it is best to listen much, speak little, and not to become angry; for anger doesn't make us good as God demands that we must be.

Amanda Adams mused over the verse. "I don't believe that anger in itself is wrong. It is a natural emotion when we feel threatened in one way or another. However, what we do with the anger is what is important. If we allow the anger to turn into revenge, resentment, negative feelings, and depression, then that is wrong. That type expression of anger doesn't make us good as God demands that we must be. If instead we turn our anger into something positive, then the anger can be healthy and good for our spiritual growth. If we express our anger in a gentle, loving way, then the air can be cleared and tension reduced. We will also feel good about ourselves because we took good care of ourselves—with God's help, of course. We must always turn to God and ask for help and guidance."

**How do you respond to anger?**

**What improvements in your approach to anger can be made?**

# October 6

Isaiah 30:21 And if you leave God's paths and go astray, you will hear a voice behind you say, "No this is the way; walk here."

Ted laughed to himself. "God, you certainly were guiding me the other day. There is something about Jeff that triggers an angry reaction in me. Every time I see the guy, I feel like punching him out. One of the bad things going against me if I take a swing is that he outweighs me by fifty pounds and is a lot taller than me. I'd be creamed. Well, the other day I came very close to taking a swing at Jeff, but I heard words in my head to the affect, 'No, this is the way; walk here.' So instead of swinging at Jeff, I laughed and walked on, ignoring him as I passed by. The problem wasn't with Jeff. The problem was my reaction to Jeff. When I laughed, I truly let what Jeff said go by. It didn't affect me. I realize that two wrongs don't make a right. I'll leave Jeff up to you, God."

**When have you felt God's guidance?**

**What happened?**

# October 7

Psalm 25:8 The Lord is good and glad to teach the proper path to all who go astray; he will teach the ways that are right and best to those who humbly turn to him.

Sara was feeling sad. "God, please guide me. I am turning to you for help because I am making myself sad by comparing myself to others. Of course when I find myself comparing, I always come out on the bottom. I am never good enough. My best isn't good enough. I then become jealous and feel down on myself. It is wrong for me to be jealous, because I then become angry and feel resentment toward the people I am jealous of. God, teach me to let go of my comparing myself to others. I realize we are all different, with different gifts and talents. Help me appreciate my gifts. Help me to be nice not only to others, but to myself as well. I turn to you because without your help, I will never become a loving person."

**Are you able to turn to the Lord asking for guidance?**

**If not, why not?**

# October 8

Tobit 4:14–15 Keep a guard, my son, on your conduct. Do not do to anyone anything you would hate to have done to you.

Sara really was feeling guilty one evening. "I really was mean to Suzanne today. She has been such a good friend to me. Why did I leave her sitting alone at the table in the cafeteria? I could have gone over to invite her to sit with the new group of friends I made. I could see that Suzanne was hurt. She has always been kind to me, and look what I did. How would I feel if Suzanne made new friends and dropped me, leaving me sitting alone at a lunch table? I'd be mad. I'd be hurt. I've been very selfish and very self-centered. I will call Suzanne tonight and tell her I am sorry. I certainly won't drop her because I have new friends. I will include her and continue my friendship with her."

**How do you want to be treated?**

**How do you treat others?**

# October 9

Isaiah 59:1 Listen now! The Lord isn't too weak to save you. And he isn't getting deaf! He can hear you when you call! But the trouble is that your sins have cut you off from God.

Jim Adams was struggling with a number of problems at work. "God, business is really getting worse, and the company is being forced to lay people off. I'm to the point where I wonder if indeed you are too weak to help out. Or are you just indifferent. I know you aren't deaf. I know you can hear my prayers. So why aren't you answering my prayers for business to improve so I won't be the next person to be laid off? I've got this family to support, and I am scared.

What are my sins, God? I do everything I can to be a good person, good husband, and father. I do everything except—oh, now I see. I do everything except let go, let you guide my life, and have trust in you. I've wanted the control instead of letting you guide my life in your way and time. My lack of trust has been cutting me off from you, God. Forgive me. Amen."

**What has kept you from feeling God's presence?**

**What has made God seem distant to you?**

# October 10

Matthew 6:3–4 But when you do a kindness to someone, do it secretly—don't tell your left hand what your right hand is doing. And your Father who knows all secrets will reward you.

Sara found the message of this verse very hard to follow. "I have this weakness of wanting people to know the kind of things I do for others. In fact, many times the reason I do nice things for others is to get compliments. Just the other day, I helped Paula with her homework. Then I went around telling everyone I met that I helped Paula. Instead of receiving any compliments or gratitude from Paula, she got mad at me instead. She told me that I embarrassed her by telling everyone I had helped her. She said it made her feel stupid and helpless. I've thought a lot about what Paula said. I was wrong in wanting credit for something I did. In the process, I hurt the person I was trying to help. I'm so sorry, God. I will tell Paula that I am sorry, also. From now on, I will be kind to others in secret, not expecting any reward at all. Thank you, God."

**When you do a kindness for someone, do you want everyone to know about it?**

**Have you ever hurt someone without meaning to?**

# October 11

Acts 18: 9–10 One night the Lord spoke to Paul in a vision and told him, "Don't be afraid! Speak out! Don't quit! For I am with you and no one can harm you. Many people here in this city belong to me."

Amanda Adams shook her head in awe. "St. Paul and the early Christians had a lot of persecution to go through. What comfort it must have been for St Paul to hear the Lord telling him not to be afraid and not to quit. The Lord reassured St. Paul that he was with him. There were many people in the city that belonged to the Lord. I really believe that if we keep ourselves open to listening to God, that like St. Paul, we too will receive encouraging insights from God. We may not have a vision like St. Paul did, but we may read scripture and receive insight or an answer. Someone may say something to us that gives us encouragement. Maybe we will hear a song that gives us an answer. God speaks to us in many ways. He is always telling us he is with us. All we have to do is listen."

**In what ways has the Lord spoken to you?**

**Do you feel he is with you?**

# October 12

Hebrews 10:35–36 Do not let this happy trust in the Lord die away, no matter what happens. Remember your reward! You need to keep on patiently doing God's will if you want him to do for you all that he has promised.

Ted wondered, "Just what is God's will? I guess he wants us to love him, to love others, and to love ourselves, also. He wants us to be joyful and to feel at peace. It is when we start fighting against things that we get off the track. It is like when I was turned down to play football this year. I was mad. I wanted revenge. I felt wronged. I didn't feel joy. I didn't feel peace, either. Finally I accepted the situation. There wasn't a thing I could do about it. I had let my trust in God fade away, and I was miserable. When I finally accepted that I wasn't going to play football this year, my anger left. I began feeling good about myself again, and I found other interests besides football. I feel joy and peace. Thank you, Lord."

**What do you think God's will is for you?**

**Have you ever let your trust in the Lord die away?**

# October 13

John 6:27 "But you shouldn't be so concerned about perishable things like food. No, spend your energy seeking the eternal life that I, the Messiah, can give you. For God, the Father, has sent me for this very purpose."

Amy was always worrying about one thing or another. "Oh God, why do I always get caught up in situations daily life brings about? I realize that things are always changing, but on one hand I am afraid of change. On the other hand, I am afraid things will never change. It seems that the positive things don't last, and the negative things never change. That of course is my own perspective. I waste energy on stewing about things that are out of my control. Instead, I should spend my energy in trying to get to know you better, Jesus. I need to build a good relationship with you. I need to remember that all I do in this life flows from my relationship with you. God sent you, Jesus, to show us the way to him. Thank you, Lord. Amen."

**Do you find yourself overly concerned about things in your life?**

**What does Jesus ask of us?**

# October 14

2 Peter 2:7–9 But at the same time the Lord rescued Lot out of Sodom because he was a good man, sick of the terrible wickedness he saw everywhere around him day after day. So also the Lord can rescue you and me from the temptations that surround us.

Amanda Adams thought about the temptations that surrounded her. "They aren't big temptations. They are the small ones that happen every day of my life; my faults that I battle day in and day out. Thank heavens I have learned to turn to God constantly during the day, asking for help in overcoming these faults. What are some of my faults? I am a perfectionist, for one thing. I want everything to be just perfect and then I'm hard on myself when things aren't. If I have a positive attitude, I feel peaceful. When I don't trust God, I try to take control of the situation. The list goes on and on. Thank you, Lord, for being there for me. You want me to let go of my useless worrying and anxiety."

**What are your temptations?**

**Do you turn to the Lord for help?**


# October 15

Romans 5:3 We can rejoice, too, when we run into problems and trials for we know that they are good for us—they help us learn to be patient. And patience develops strength of character in us and helps us trust God more each time we use it.

Jim Adams agreed that having problems and trials are actually good for him. "I sure don't like to have problems. But each time problems have come along, I can look back and see how much I grew in my faith once I decided to trust in God. This job situation is a trial, but I am beginning to sense that this is a time for me to look for a new job. I am scared because it will be a big change, and maybe a loss of income, yet maybe it will be a very positive change. It won't be easy, but having a positive attitude, which comes from a trust in God, will help me be patient. It will certainly build my character. Today I was told about a job opening, so I will follow up on it and any other openings that come up. Be with me, Lord."

**Are you patient in times of trials?**

**Have you, with God's help, become more patient?**

# October 16

1 Corinthians 3:20 And again, in the book of Psalms, we are told that the Lord knows full well how the human mind reasons, and how foolish and futile it is.

Amy drove herself silly sometimes trying to figure out what scripture meant. "It's really open to many interpretations, which has divided people and religions during the course of history. I have run into people who quote scripture every time they want to prove a point. All I can say is that I have faith. I accept the mystery of faith. I know I will never be able to figure out what God is about. It would indeed be foolish and futile for me to try. Yes, God, I know you know how our human minds do reason. That is why you only ask of us to love you, love our neighbor, and love ourselves. You want to have a relationship with us, and that is all we really need to know. Help me continue to accept the mysteries of my faith. Amen."

**How does your mind reason?**

**Are you able to accept God's mysteries?**

# October 17

Galatians 6:4–5 Let everyone be sure that he is doing his very best, for then he will have the personal satisfaction of work well done, and won't need to compare himself with someone else. Each of us must bear some faults and burdens of our own. For none of us is perfect.

Sara hoped she was doing her best in school. "I've been comparing myself to some of my friends lately, and that makes me unhappy. Maybe I am not actually doing my best. Well, I am trying to do my best, but in math I am finding some things hard to understand. I am afraid to ask my teacher for help. I pretend I understand, hoping to fool everyone. I don't want them to think I am dumb. Well, the verse says that none of us is perfect, so my not understanding math is okay. My fault is that I don't want to ask Mrs. Wells for help. That is wrong of me, isn't it? If I continue to make low grades, Mrs. Wells will know I don't understand, anyway. She will respect me if I ask her for help before I make low grades. Help me, God, to find the courage to ask. Amen."

**Do you feel satisfaction from doing work the best way you can?**

**Are you able to ask for help when you don't understand?**

# October 18

Luke 11:28 He replied, "Yes, but even more blessed are all who hear the Word of God and put it into practice."

Ted was thinking about the weekend plans that the guys were making. "Jeff's parents are going to be out of town this weekend, so Jeff is going to throw a party at his house. I really want to go because it sounds like fun. Yet I know how arrogant Jeff can be. He has been into a lot of drinking lately, and with a few beers, he becomes even more arrogant. His party could turn into a big mess. I heard that the police had to be called the last time he threw a party. My gut feeling tells me to put my time to better use. What do you think I should do, God? Yes, I know. I have heard your Word. To put it into practice, it is best to stay away from Jeff's party. Mom and Dad will certainly be relieved to hear about my decision. Thank you, God."

**Do you put God's Word into practice?**

**In what ways?**

# October 19

Psalm 71:17–18 O God, you have helped me from my earliest child-hood—and I have constantly testified to the wonderful things you do. And now that I am old and gray, don't forsake me.

Amanda Adams thought of her conversation she had with her mother, who said, "Amanda, I feel so frustrated at times. Just about everything I was taught was right while growing up I am now told is wrong. My values are old-fashioned. There have been a lot of positive changes since I was young, but along with the positive are some very negative changes. The one thing I have learned is to rely completely on God for his guidance. Only God knows what is good and right for each of us. Of course, a person should seek advice from other people to help discern what is right for each of us, but other people's judgments are not much better than our own. The best thing to do is to go to scripture and of course, go to church. If we do that, we won't feel forsaken now or when we are old and gray."

**Have you ever felt forsaken by God?**

**Have you ever felt forsaken by people?**

# October 20

James 1:26 Anyone who says he is a Christian but doesn't control his sharp tongue is just fooling himself, and his religion isn't worth much.

Amy had been struggling with how to stand up for herself, her needs, and her wants. She wanted to get her point of view across without making other people angry. "So far, all I seem to do when I put my point across to others is create negative reactions. I seem to sway between being passive to being aggressive. I guess that is because when I am passive, I am not recognizing my need to express my point of view. Then I go to the extreme and become very aggressive because I feel angry. Help me, God, to be assertive. Help me to express my viewpoints in a polite and respectful way. I want to learn the skill of assertion to show that I do love you, God, love others, and love myself. Only with your grace will I be able to be assertive.

**Are you able to express your needs and wants in a polite, assertive way?**

**What is the difference between being assertive or aggressive?**

# October 21

Amos 5:4 The Lord says to the people of Israel, "Seek me and live. Don't seek the idols of Bethel, Gilgal, or Berr-sheba; for the people of Gilgal will be carried off to exile and those of Bethel shall surely come to grief."

Jim Adams thought back to the time of his childhood. "When I was a kid, I thought idols were other Gods such as the Roman gods and goddesses. It wasn't until I was an adult that I realized that idols weren't necessarily other deities. I found that I had more than my share of idols that came between God and me. In fact, I learned that anything that does come between God and me is an idol. I had the idols of my concern about my finances, my career, my tendency to overeat, and my fear of failure. The list goes on and on. Money, pride, power, and all of my negative emotions that come between God and me are idols. Those idols bring grief and slavery. Everyday, God, I need to examine what is in my mind. I need to examine all of my motives. I need to ask for your help in freeing me from these idols."

**What are your idols?**

**What do you need to do to be free of these idols?**

# October 22

Sirach (Ecclesiastics) 2:6 Believe God and he will strengthen you and direct your way. Trust in him. Be reverent to him and grow old in his ways.

Ted had been getting pretty lazy in thinking about God. "I've gotten so caught up in hanging out with my friends that God has seemed pretty far away. I have been just going through the motions to please Mom and Dad. Do I really believe you, God? Do I really believe in you? Yes, I believe in you and in what you say. I know you give me strength, and I know you direct my way. Do I trust you? Yes, I do. Am I very reverent to you, God? Not as much as I should be. You are my everything. Without you and your graces, I am nothing. I need your help and guidance. Without your help, I quickly get off the right path. God, I want to grow old in your ways. I realize that I can still hang out with my friends if I will take you, God, along in my heart. Thank you."

**Do you feel reverent towards God?**

**Are you growing old in his ways?**

# October 23

Wisdom 15:1,3 But you, our God, are kind, true, patient, and ruling all things in mercy. For to know you is perfect justice, and to know your justice and your might is the root of eternal life.

Sara loved this image of God. "How I wish I could be like that. I wish I could always be true, kind, patient, and forgiving. If I could have all of those qualities all the time, then I could be a person who is always filled with God's peace. The more I learn about God and his love, the more I will want to have his qualities of love and forgiveness. I need your guidance, God. Without your help I will miss the mark in being a person filled with truth, patience, kindness, and forgiveness. I cannot have these qualities through my own efforts. Knowing your justice and your power is the root of eternal life. Knowing you is the way. I love you, God. Thank you for your truth, mercy, patience, and kindness. Amen."

**Are you a person of truth, kindness, patience, and forgiveness?**

**If you miss the mark, how can you get on the right path?**

# October 24

1 Corinthians 3:18–19 Stop fooling yourselves. If you count yourself above average in intelligence, as judged by this world's standards, you had better put this all aside and be a fool rather than let it hold you back from true wisdom from above.

Ted had been feeling pretty smug about his A average in school. "Maybe I had better rethink feeling cocky about my good grades. I don't know why, but schoolwork has always come easily to me. I didn't think much about it until this year when I was elected president of the Honor Society. When I didn't make the football team, I turned to my studies to make me feel I was better than other people. I didn't realize I was doing that until just now. I am not better than anyone else. We all have our own individual talents. Bringing all of our talents together for the common good is like having wisdom from above. When we use our talents as ego trips, we become separated from each other. When we don't use our talents for the common good, we take the wrong path. Help keep me on the right path, God."

**What are your talents?**

**Do you spread God's word using your talents?**

# October 25

John 21:17 Once more he asked him, "Simon, son of John, are you even my friend?" Peter was grieved at the way Jesus asked the question this third time. "Lord you know my heart; you know I am," he said.

Sally imagined Jesus asking her, "Sally, daughter of Jim, are you even my friend?"

"I guess Jesus had asked Peter this question three times, and I guess Peter felt bad that Jesus didn't seem to think he was his friend. Would Jesus have to ask me three times? I guess there are many times that I don't act like I am a friend to Jesus. I am a friend to Suzanne, but sometimes I don't act like I am her friend. When I don't act like Suzanne's friend, I am not acting like I am Jesus' friend. When I treat Suzanne badly, I am treating Jesus bad. When I treat anyone in a bad way, I am treating Jesus in a bad way. When I talk about others in a bad way, then I am talking about Jesus in a bad way. The way I treat others is the way I treat Jesus. Help me be your friend, Jesus. Amen."

**How do you treat others?**

**How do you treat Jesus?**

# October 26

John 15:4 "Take care to live in me, and let me live in you. For a branch can't produce fruit where severed from the vine. Nor can you be fruitful apart from me."

Jim Adams knew how true this verse was in his life. "Apart from Jesus, I certainly didn't produce good fruit. My life became complicated and my energies were scattered. It got to the point that I began to ask the question of 'is this all there is?' I had it made according to the world's standard. I had a good job, a wonderful wife, and wonderful children. I had more than enough of the material things that life can offer, but I was feeling empty. Then I began attending church with Amanda and the kids, and I found myself searching for God's wisdom. It was like a miracle. My life became meaningful. There was a purpose to it. I came to appreciate the mystery of God's love, and I thank God for making my life so rich."

**Have you ever asked the question "Is this all there is?"**

**Do you ever feel cut off from the vine?**

# October 27

Jeremiah 17: 5–6 The Lord says: Cursed is the man, who puts his trust in mortal man and turns his heart away from God. He is like a stunted shrub in the desert, with no hope for the future; he lives on the salt encrusted plains in the barren wilderness; good times pass him by forever.

Amy felt that these two verses spoke to her in a very deep way. "I find myself always wanting to follow popular people and the latest fads. I want to do everything my peer group is doing. Well, almost everything. There are a number of things my peer group does that

I know would leave me like a stunted shrub in the desert. Some of the kids my age have become addicted to drugs, and their lives have become a torment for them. That scares me. Others are led around by the popular thing to do. Their hearts are turned away from God. It is so easy to follow the ways of the world, but in doing so, the good times pass them by because they don't know what the good times really are."

**Have you ever trusted in mortal man?**

**What happened?**

# October 28

Psalm 16:8–9 I am always thinking of the Lord; and because he is so near, I never need to stumble or to fall. Heart, body, and soul are filled with joy.

Amanda Adams reflected back on the times she felt that to be with God, she needed to visit a church. "How could I have felt that the only place I would find God was in a church? But I did feel that way. Then one day, I realized that God was in my heart, and therefore, he is with me at all times. He is nearer to me than I am to myself. My thoughts are constantly aware of his presence within me. Even during the times of my life when I feel God is very far away, I know he is really near. The knowledge of his nearness brings me joy, even in the midst of troubles and sorrow. All I need to do is ask for the courage and the strength to have trust that everything will turn out okay in God's way and in God's timing. Thank you, God, for being in my heart."

**Do you feel that God is in your heart?**

**If not, why?**

# October 29

James 1: 13–14 And remember, when someone wants to do wrong it is never God who is tempting him, for God never wants to do wrong and never tempts anyone else to do it. Temptation is the pull of man's own evil thoughts and wishes.

Ted knew this was the truth. "God doesn't lead us into temptation. We need to pray for God's strength, courage, and guidance to help us realize when we are on a bad course of action. Asking for God's help will keep us from being led into temptation. I know I have to battle my pride. There is a difference between having pride and having self-confidence. Pride is feeling I am better than others. It can lead to negative competition. Self-confidence is a knowing that I am okay and others are okay, too. Each and every day, I am tempted to compare myself with others, which leads to the destructive feelings of being better than others or not good enough."

**What are your temptations?**

**How can God help you to resist these temptations?**

# October 30

Leviticus 19:18 Don't seek vengeance. Don't bear a grudge; but love your neighbor as yourself, for I am Jehovah.

Amanda Adams was surprised to find this verse in the old testament. "I always think of Jesus and the new testament saying love your neighbor as yourself. I always think of the old testament saying an eye for an eye and a tooth for a tooth. How healthy it is for a person to love his neighbor as himself by not seeking vengeance and not holding a grudge. Why is it healthy? It is healthy because seeking vengeance and holding grudges harm us by taking away our own peace and joy. We harm ourselves. Our lives can become filled with anger and bitterness. What does our vengeance and grudge holding do to the other person? Probably not much of anything in comparison to what it does to us. God, I ask your help in dealing with any anger I have in helping me not to turn it into vengeance and grudge holding. Amen."

**Have you ever wanted revenge or have you ever held a grudge?**

**What did these feelings do to your peace of mind?**

# October 31

Joel 2:13 "Return to the Lord your God, for he is gracious and merciful. He is not easily angered; he is full of kindness, and anxious not to punish you."

Jim Adams thought back on his elementary school years. "I was very afraid of God then. I was told that whenever I did something against the Ten Commandments, God would punish me. I did not want to be punished by God, so I tried very hard to keep all the rules. I finally decided I wasn't good enough for God and strayed away from God and my church. I later learned that God loves us all very much; so much that he sent his Son, Jesus, to become one of us. Jesus is the bridge between us and God. Yes, I believe that God is gracious and merciful. He is anxious not to punish us. Actually, we punish ourselves when we break the Ten Commandments. Why? The result of negative choices is a negative result. It is all cause and effect. Help me to make positive choices, God. Thank you. Amen."

**Has God been gracious and merciful to you?**

**What negative choices in your life brought on negative results?**

# November

# November 1

Ezekiel 33:11 Tell them: As I live, says the Lord God, I have no pleasure in the death of the wicked; I desire that the wicked turn from his evil ways and live.

Amy pondered this verse in her mind. "This is a powerful verse for me. Is God saying that he doesn't take pleasure in seeing a wicked person receive punishment? Evil brings death to a person's soul. God wants us to be whole people and to live life in his peace and joy. He wants the wicked people to turn from their evil ways and become whole and filled with God's life. Sometimes a view of God is given that sounds like God is filled with anger and rage at wicked people. What a soul-killing message that is. God desires the wicked to turn from evil and live, which is a life-giving message. Thank you, God, for your love. Amen."

**Are you becoming a person who is one-step at a time truly living in God's life giving ways?**

**Where are your weaknesses?**

# November 2

Amos 5:14 Be good, flee evil—and live! Then the Lord God of Hosts will truly be your Helper, as you have claimed he is.

Ted wondered if he really was on the right track in his decisions.

"Being a teenager is hard. So many new things come into my life each day—new thoughts, new feelings, and many times new attitudes. I am trying to choose the right path, and I am trying hard to flee evil. However, there are times when evil is disguised as appearing good. How does a person tell the difference? I suppose it is from the results of the actions one takes. For instance, if I want to take good care of my body by exercising and weight control, that is good. But if I get out of balance and exercise to excess, and either eat too much or too little, then I am doing myself harm or evil. I guess my prayer to you, God, is that I want to be good. I need your help to flee evil, and you have said you would give me your help. Thank you. Amen."

**When have you thought you were doing well and it ended up being bad?**

**Where was God in all of this?**

# November 3

Psalm 19: 9–11 God's laws are pure, eternal, just. They are more desirable than gold. They are sweeter than honey dripping from a honeycomb. For they warn us away from harm.

Sally was learning about the Ten Commandments in religion class. "That is what Mrs. Phipps told us about God's laws. She said that if we follow the Ten Commandments, we would be on the right path. If we follow the laws, we will be kept away from harm. I know that when I do something wrong, such as telling a lie, then I am on the wrong path. I know this because the Ten Commandments tell us not to tell lies. When I talk back in a rude way to Mom and Dad, I am not showing love and respect, and that breaks one of God's laws. If I would take some money that belongs to Mom and Dad without asking them, I would be stealing, and that is against God's law. The list goes on forever of things I could do that are wrong, so I pay attention to the Ten Commandments, which keep me from harm."

**How do you feel about God's laws?**

**Have they kept you out of harm's way?**

# November 4

Psalm 25: 4–5 Show me the path where I should go, O Lord' point out the right road for me to walk. Lead me; teach me; for you are the God who gives me salvation. I have no hope except in you.

Jim Adams nodded his head in agreement. "God, I say these two verses everyday before I start the day. They are the foundation of my life. You are the foundation of my life. I am nothing without your help. I can do nothing without your help. I need the right road pointed out to me many times during each day. I need your guidance in everything I do. I need you to teach me and to lead me when I am with my children. I want to be a loving Father to them. I want to be a good parent. I can't be this good parent without your loving wisdom. I feel so weak; yet like St. Paul, I do feel your strength working in my weakness. Please help my children to realize that they need your teachings and wisdom to guide them through life.

**Is God the foundation of your life?**

**What are some of your weaknesses?**

# November 5

Luke 4: 18–19 "The Spirit of the Lord is upon me; he has appointed me to preach good news to the poor; he has sent me to heal the broken-hearted and to announce that captives shall be released and the blind shall see."

Amanda Adams reflected back to the time she didn't fully understand about the good news. "I must admit that I didn't think that Jesus had anything to say to me. After all, I wasn't brokenhearted, and I certainly wasn't a captive; nor was I blind. Then one day I did become brokenhearted and realized that I was a captive of my grief. With prayer, my blindness to God's love and mercy ended, and I could then see his love with my new sight. All of us will become brokenhearted, captive, and blind. The good news is that God is here in each of our hearts to free us from our bondage. All we need to do is to become aware of his presence and invite him into our lives. Thank you, God, for your tender love. Amen."

**Have you ever been brokenhearted, captive, or blind?**

**What happened?**

# November 6

Psalm 36: 9–10 For you are the Fountain of life; our light is from your Light. Pour out your unfailing love on those who know you! Never stop giving your salvation to those who long to do your will.

Amy was tutoring one of her classmates who was having a problem learning Spanish. "I was so excited when I was asked to tutor Lilly. I knew she was having problems with Spanish, and I love to help people. I have made six appointments to meet with Lilly, and she has kept only two of those six appointments. She asked me to call her to remind her of our appointments. She stood me up once and had an excuse for not keeping the other three. God, I feel so confused. I feel that Lilly doesn't want me to help her. I guess I feel her not wanting my help will reflect on me as not having good helping skills. My pride is showing up here, isn't it? Plus, I should have never allowed her to insist that I call her to remind her of the appointments. God, I want to do your will. Please help me see your light. Amen."

**Do you long to do God's will?**

**In what ways has he helped you to do so?**

# November 7

Psalm 107:8–9 Oh, that these men would praise the Lord for his loving kindness, and for all his wondrous deeds! For he satisfies the thirsty soul and fills the hungry soul with good.

Amanda Adams certainly agreed with these verses. "I don't really thank you enough for all of the many things you have given us—yet, I'm quick to tell you, God, what you haven't done. I believe that I am that way with others also. I don't tell people what they are doing that is good, but I am quick to point out their mistakes. My soul is thirsty for your wisdom. I need your help in gracing me with love and compassion for others. I know that already you have filled up my hungry soul with good, but it will take a lifetime for my soul to be satisfied. I appreciate and thank you, God, for your love, compassion, and kindness. Help me show mercy to others. Amen."

**Is your soul thirsty?**

**Is your soul being filled with good?**

# November 8

Psalm 27: 7–8 Listen to my pleading Lord! Be merciful and send the help I need. My heart has heard you say, "Come and talk with me, O my people." And my heart responds, "Lord, I am coming."

Sara didn't eat very much dinner. She felt so very sad. "God, I didn't make the honor roll at school because I received a D in Physical Education. The D kept me off the honor roll. I can't help it if I am not able to throw a ball very far, run very fast, jump very high, or turn a cartwheel. I try so hard, God, but my body just won't cooperate. I feel like I have a serious handicap because I am not very good at sports. God, I am sitting here talking to you. I know that you listen to me. What are you saying in reply? Oh, you are saying that I have many other talents that I can use. Not everyone can be good in sports. In fact, this might be put to good use in realizing what others might feel like when they don't measure up to what society expects. I am learning empathy."

**Is there something that you feel handicapped in?**

**Has a handicap taught you to have empathy?**

# November 9

Matthew 5:7 "Happy are the kind and merciful, for they shall be shown mercy."

Amy wondered what the word mercy meant. "Does it mean to forgive and to feel pity for another person? The other day, Art got really mad during recess. He is a pretty fast runner. He and Joe were having a race, and Joe won. Art was furious because he lost. He went up to Joe and hit him in the face. It was a shock to Joe, who just stood there and looked Art straight in the eye. There was silence, and then Joe put his hand on Art's shoulder and said, "Let's talk about it." They both walked off talking as Art kicked at rocks along the way. Later in the day, I could see that Art and Joe's friendship was stronger than ever. Joe showed mercy to Art. Joe could have hit Art back, but he chose to be kind and merciful. This is what God wants us to do. Showing kindness and mercy to each other is doing God's will."

**When have you been shown kindness and mercy?**

**How does this make you feel?**

# November 10

Hebrews 4:15 This High Priest of ours understands ours weaknesses, since he had the same temptations we do, though he never once gave way to them and sinned.

Ted thought about all of his weaknesses. "Surely Jesus didn't have weaknesses or temptations. He was God's son. How could he have temptations? But he did. Right after he was baptized, Satan tempted him with thoughts appealing to the weaknesses of every human. What did Jesus do? He turned to scripture. Jesus did not give in. He did not sin. Nonetheless, he still felt the pain of having those weak spots, so he does know how we feel. He promises to save us from these temptations if we but only turn to him and ask for his help. It is wonderful having a High Priest who does understand us. Thank you, God, for sending your son to share our humanity with us. Amen."

**What are your weaknesses?**

**Do you ask God to help you overcome these weaknesses?**

# November 11

Psalm 33: 4–5 For all God's words are right, and everything he does is worthy of our trust. He loves whatever is just and good; the earth is filled with his tender love.

"Another world crisis is dominating the news," thought Amanda Adams. "No matter where I went today, radios or TVs blared out about the problems this crisis was creating. So once again, we are all obsessing on the latest evil to hit the earth. Good news is seldom heard. Most news is negative, and we humans seem to dwell on what is wrong with this world. We don't spend much time thanking God for all the just and good things in the world. Yes, there is evil in the world, but there is a lot of good. We need to keep in touch with the good so that we can feel God's love and see how he is so worthy of our trust. God, you are nothing but goodness. Thank you. Amen."

**Do you obsess on the negative things of the world?**

**What are you grateful for? Do you thank God for these blessings?**


# November 12

James 1:13–14 And remember, when someone wants to do wrong it is never God who is tempting him, for God never wants to do wrong and never tempts anyone else to do it.

Jim Adams reflected back on a conversation he had with his friend, Jerry. "What a time of struggle Jerry has been going through. Most of the struggle has been of Jerry's own doing. Life had been going smoothly for Jerry, but he was feeling bored. He wanted to do many things that even a year ago he would never have thought of. Jerry's excuse was he felt that God was tempting him with all of these negative activities, but I tried to explain to him that I didn't feel that any of this was coming from God. It was coming from Jerry's own lack of gratitude for the many blessings he already had. So he became bored with life. God, watch over Jerry. Give him the wisdom and the courage to let go of this man-made struggle and instead give you thanks for his blessings. Amen."

**Have you ever become bored with your life?**

**What happened?**

# November 13

Psalm 37:8 Stop your anger! Turn off your wrath. Don't fret and worry—it only leads to harm.

Ted knew he was angry again. "Why is it I can not seem to control my temper? I know that it is a natural human emotion to become angry at times, but I don't know what to do with my own anger. I either strike out in a hot temper, or I simmer in a pot of worry and fretfulness. I lose all of my God given peace, that's for sure. I find that I want to harm the person I am mad at. I want revenge. That is harmful not only to the person I am mad at, but to me as well. Actually, I know I do more harm to myself. God, what am I going to do with this hot temper of mine? Please guide me. I want to change. I want to learn communication skills. I want to change my attitudes. I don't want to be on the defensive. I trust you to help me. Thank you, God. Amen."

**How do you behave when you are angry?**

**What are some of your attitudes? Are you sometimes on the defensive?**

# November 14

Joel 2:13 Return to the Lord your God for he is gracious and merciful.

Amy was thinking about Eric. "It seems like yesterday that Eric was getting in and out of trouble. His parents were heartsick with worry, and so were we, his friends. Eric had a great personality, and everyone liked him until he got hooked on drugs. It was a shock to all of us. As time went on, we saw less and less of Eric. We missed him and prayed that one day soon, he would see the light and get help for his drug addiction. Our prayers were answered, and Eric hit the so-called bottom. He couldn't go on living the way he was, and he agreed to go to a treatment center. I often thought about God while Eric was in treatment. How could God help Eric and I realize that God is gracious and merciful? Eric was taken over by drugs, and with God's help, Eric will get back on track and come alive once again. I saw Eric the other day, and he said he was taking life one day at a time."

**When in your life have you found God to be gracious and merciful?**

**Are you gracious and merciful toward others?**

# November 15

Psalm 51:10 Create me a new, clean heart, O God, filled with clean thoughts and right desires.

Sara had been fighting a wave of jealousy the past few days. "Why do I feel so jealous of Marilyn? I don't understand it. Everyone loves being her friend. She always has a group of people around her. All of the teachers think she is great, also. She is the school's little darling. She is pretty, makes good grades, has pretty clothes, and a great personality. So what do I have in comparison? Well, I have friends, but not as many as she has. The teachers like me, but not as much as Marilyn. I make fairly good grades but not as high as hers. I have nice clothes, but not as pretty as hers. My personality is okay, but not like hers. God, I am comparing myself to Marilyn and not giving you thanks for the many blessings you have given to me. Please create in me a new, clean heart of thanksgiving and grateful thoughts. Give me the right desire of being grateful for whom I am and grateful for whom Marilyn is. Thank you, God."

**Have you ever been jealous of another person?**

**Why? What were the results of these jealous feelings?**

# November 16

Baruch 3:6–7 You are the Lord our God, and we will praise you, O Lord, since you have put your respect in our hearts to help us call upon your name.

Amanda Adams gave some thought to this verse. "This is an interesting verse. Yes, God, we will praise you. We do praise you. It sounds like the verse is saying that you have given us the grace, which is your respect, in our hearts. Because of this grace, we are helped to call on you. You love us, and because you love us, you want to have a relationship with us. The gift of grace is always there. However, you do give us the freedom to receive your grace-filled love into our lives. The choice is ours to make. The choice is between peace in the midst of our daily lives or anxiety and restlessness in the midst of our daily lives. I accept your grace-filled love. Thank you. Amen."

**Do you praise the Lord no matter what is happening in your life?**

**Do you accept his gift of grace-filled peace?**

# November 17

Ezekiel 33:11 As I live, says the Lord God, I have no pleasure in the death of the wicked; I desire that the wicked turn from his evil ways and live.

Amy mused to herself, thinking the verse over. "God, of course you don't take any pleasure in punishing the wicked. Of course you want the wicked to turn away from his evil ways and live. You are the God of love. You are love. It must break your heart when people become wicked. Not only do wicked people harm themselves, but they harm others as well. So much heartache is caused by the wicked. You are indeed the God of love, not revenge. Much of the time, it turns out that the wicked harm themselves by bringing on their own punishment. It is the law of cause and effect. If you touch a hot stove, the effect will be that you get burned. God, thank you for being the God of love. Amen."

**Do you believe that God is the God of love?**

**When you have done something wrong, what have been the results of that wrong action?**

# November 18

Psalm 86: 6–7 Listen closely to my prayer, O God. Hear my urgent cry. I will call to you whenever trouble strikes, and you will help me.

Sally had a bad day at school. "Mrs. Wells asked for volunteers to make Thanksgiving Day decorations for the classroom. When I raised my hand, she chose everyone but me. She totally ignored me. I guess she doesn't think I draw or color very well. God, what did I do wrong? Why doesn't she want me to help her anymore? She used to call on me all the time, but lately she doesn't ask me to do a thing.

God, please help me know the reason. Oh, yes, now I think I know why she hasn't called on me. Already I am doing a lot of extra things for the classroom. I guess she is giving the other kids a chance to do their share of volunteering to give them the experience. I've been a volunteer hog. Now it's someone else's turn. Thank you, God, for the answer. I feel better now. Amen."

**Do you call on God when trouble strikes?**

**Does he answer your prayers?**

# November 19

Psalm 19: 12–13 But how can I ever know what sins are lurking in my heart? Cleanse me from these hidden faults. And keep me from deliberate wrongs; help me to stop doing them.

Jim Adams mulled these words over in his mind. "Cleanse me from these hidden faults, hidden sins. What are my hidden faults? I am impatient. I ask you, God, to help me be patient not only with others, but with myself as well. Perfection—I want to be perfect. Do I want others to be perfect also? Perfect in my eyes, of course. Does this perfection lead me to be judgmental of others as well as myself? Does a hidden fault or sin actually mean that we become out of balance? Say, trying to do the best we can actually can be taken too far, thereby becoming out of balance, which then becomes the fault or sin of perfectionism. The list of faults can go on and on in the scheme of being out of balance in our daily living. God, help me keep my life in balance by focusing on you. Amen."

**What are your hidden faults?**

**Is your daily life in balance or out of balance?**

# November 20

Hosea 6:6 I don't want your sacrifices—I want your love; I don't want your offerings—I want you to know me.

Jake was so happy to be back home from college for the Thanksgiving break. "I have really kept focused on this verse these past months at school. I have tried to be open to God's love and friendship in the midst of the noise of the dorm, studying, and the social life of college. It's been hard at times to know how to keep the balance between studying and socializing. When my grades dropped after the first few weeks at school, I learned fast that I had to crack the books more often. I also started going to the library for some quiet time for studying. Being at school, I am getting to know you, God, through many new ways and new people. However, the foundation of my relationship with you started here with my family at this dinner table. Thank you for this gift. Amen."

**Does God have your love?**

**Do you feel that you are learning to know God?**

# November 21

Psalm 31:7 I am radiant with joy because of your mercy, for you have listened to my troubles and have seen the crisis in my soul.

Amy was silently crying, "God, please listen to Bev's troubles. She has run away from home again. I wish there was something I could do to help Bev deal with her family, but there isn't anything I can do except listen to her. She has been going to a support group and talking to a social worker, but it doesn't seem to be enough. I don't know what will happen to her soul. I place Bev into your loving care. I hand her over to you. If I can be of help to her, I know you will give me guidance and tell me the best way I can help. In the meantime, I will keep Bev in my heart and my prayers, knowing she is in your care. Amen."

**Do you believe that God is able to see the crisis in our souls?**

**Does God listen to our troubles?**

# November 22

1 Thessalonians 5: 17–18 Always keep on praying. No matter what happens, always be thankful, for this is God's will for you who belong to Christ Jesus.

Amanda Adams did feel so thankful. "God, I am so grateful to you for giving Jim and me these wonderful children who share the table with us this Thanksgiving Day. It's so great having Jake back home for a few days. He has adjusted so well to college life. Amy and Ted are doing so well in high school. Sara has had a hard time adjusting to seventh grade, but she is doing better. Of course Sara loves the first grade. The children are developing a deep faith in you, God. I am so grateful for your grace-filled gifts. God, I know that there are going to be upsetting times as well as the good times. I realize that no matter what happens, I will always keep on praying. I will always be thankful because this is your will for me. Amen."

**What are you thankful for?**

**What do you think God's will is for you?**

# November 23

Philippians 2: 15–16 You are to live clean, innocent lives as children of God in a dark world full of people who are crooked and stubborn. Shine out among them like beacon lights, holding out to them the Word of Life.

Jim Adams had been watching the evening news before dinner and came to the table with sadness for the world. "God, there are truly people who are crooked and stubborn in this hate-filled world. The news of the world gets worse with each passing year. Of course this has been the case since Adam and Eve. God, you ask us humans to live clean innocent lives as children of God in this world of darkness. You ask us to shine out into the darkness, showing the way to your truth, wisdom, and love. To do this God—to be a beacon of light in this dark world—I need your help. I am too frail to be this light strictly on my own. I need your truth, wisdom, and love. God, please grace me with your protection. Amen."

**How do you view the world?**

**How can you be a beacon of light in a dark world?**

# November 24

1 John 4:12 For though we have never yet seen God, when we love each other, God lives in us and his love within us grows ever stronger.

Amy wished many times that she could see God. "I know that God is always near me, but sometimes I do wish I could see him. Then I realize that I need to have faith, which believes without seeing. When I love others, then God does live in me, and this love in me then grows stronger. I suppose I could explain this with a triangle. God loves me, I love my neighbor, and my neighbor loves God. Then I can work back in the triangle with God loves my neighbor, my neighbor loves me, and I love God. Love is the key to peace. It is not a possessive type of love, which really isn't love at all. I'm thinking about a selfless love, a caring love, a forgiving love, a freeing love, and a non-controlling kind of love—a God-like love. Help me grow into this God-like love, God. Amen."

**Do you wish you could see God?**

**What kind of faith do you have?**

# November 25

Psalm 101:2 I will try to walk a blameless path, but how I need your help, especially in my own home, where I long to act as I should.

Ted sighed to himself. "What is wrong with me this Thanksgiving weekend? Is it because Jake is home from college and I am mad about all the attention he is getting? Or am I mad that I am in high school instead of college like him? Am I mad that he is free to come and go as he pleases, but I am not old enough to have a driver's license yet? Yes, God, I sure do need your help, especially in my own home. All I have done is either sulk or pick a fight with anyone I come in contact with. I hate to admit it, but I can hardly wait for Jake to leave today for school. Of course he will be back for Christmas break in a couple of weeks. God, I don't want to feel this way. I love my brother. Maybe I am just plain mad because Jake hasn't had much to say to me. Well, it's no wonder, with me always coming back with smart talk instead of conversation. Be with us, God. Amen.

**Do you try to walk a blameless path?**

**Do you need God's help?**

# November 26

Psalm 94:19 Lord, when doubts fill my mind, when my heart is in turmoil, quiet me and give me renewed hope and cheer.

Amy did not enjoy Thanksgiving weekend all that much. "It's funny how much we all wanted to be together as a complete family, but we have all changed in many little ways since Jake left for school. Ted acted mad the whole visit. Dad and Mom were extremely happy, yet I know there was tension in the air. Sara was quieter than usual. Sally was into the Thanksgiving stories and all, so she was fine. I just felt sort of sad. Nothing was really the same. I began doubting myself and my family because things had changed. I did feel turmoil in my heart. I turned to you, and I realized in my heart that nothing does stay the same. We are in constant change. We have choice to grow with the changes or to be said that things are not the same. I choose to grow with your renewed hope and cheer in my heart."

**How do you feel about change?**

**Do you choose to grow?**

# November 27

Wisdom 1: 1–2 Think of the Lord with goodness and seek him with simplicity of heart, because he is found by those who do not tempt him, and he shows himself to those who have faith in him.

Jim Adams pondered these words. "What does it mean to seek God with simplicity of heart? Does it mean coming to terms with all the questions we have going unanswered? We cry out our 'whys' and our cry goes unanswered. Does it mean surrendering to the fact that there are no answers? Does it mean God's thoughts are not our thoughts? Does it mean accepting the mysteries and rejoicing in them? Is this the essence of faith? I think so. This is a child like faith, this simplicity of heart. God, I need your grace to bring me to this surrender and to acceptance of the mysteries. I have faith that your grace will bring me to this surrender. Amen."

**Are you yet comfortable with the unanswered questions?**

**Do you have simplicity of heart?**

# November 28

Psalm 131: 1–3 Lord, I am not proud and haughty. I don't think myself better than others. I don't pretend to "know it all." I am quiet now before the Lord, just as a child who is weaned from the breast. Yes, my begging has been stilled.

Amanda Adams thought back on the Thanksgiving weekend. "I realize that my family is changing. As each member grows, I must let go of and encourage them to stand on their own two feet. I must pray for your grace to be able to do so. I am very proud of my family, and each member is a pretty special person. I've been there to help, but it's not my doing—it is your guidance working through Jim and me. When I was a new mother, I was constantly begging for your help for even the smallest thing. That was good because it helped build a relationship with you. Now, however, I do feel like a child who has been weaned. My begging has been stilled and I am quiet before you. I sit in silence with you. I share time alone with you, God, knowing all will be well. Thank you, God. Amen."

**Are you able to sit quietly with the Lord?**

**Are you able to trust the Lord?**

# November 29

Amos 5:14 Be good, flee evil—live! Then the Lord God of Hosts will truly be your helper as you have claimed he is.

Sara wondered if she really was a good person. "I try to be good, God. I get so upset, though, when things don't go my way, like when Jake was home. I was glad to see him, but my gosh, you would think he was some kind of celebrity being a big college boy home from school. Oh, God, I am sorry. I am feeling jealous once again, aren't I? 'Second Place' is my name. Stay quiet and just smile. Everyone else is more important than you are, Sara. Oh, God, I know in my head that is not true, but in my heart I feel like my name is 'Second Place.' I guess these thoughts in my heart aren't good for me, are they, God? I am the one calling myself 'Second Place,' aren't I? You love me, God, and I know you will give me the grace to flee these negative thoughts so I can feel your peace and joy. Amen."

**Have you ever felt your name was "Second Place"?**

**Does God call you "First Place" or "Second Place" in his heart? Why?**

# November 30

James 1:21 So get rid of all that is wrong in your life, both inside and outside, and humbly be glad for the wonderful message we have received, for it is able to save our souls as it takes hold of our hearts.

Jim Adams remembered back to a time in his life when plenty was wrong both inside and outside. "Thank you, God, for being with me in all that struggle. You didn't seem to be around at all; not that I even gave you a thought, nor did I even care to think of you. I look back now, and I can see how much you were indeed a part of my life, and how much you were sharing my struggle. I fought against you until one day I realized that I was not in control of anything, including my own life, so I humbly handed my life over to your care. How my life changed. How everything fell into place one-step at a time. Thank you, God. Thank you."

Have you ever been at a place when you realized that you are not in control of your life?

**Who do you allow to be in control of your life? God? Yourself? Or others?**

# 12 December

## December 1

Isaiah 35:4 Encourage those who are afraid. Tell them: Be strong, fear not for your God is coming to destroy your enemies. He is coming to save you.

Sally was so excited about the beginning of the holiday season. "I have been getting ready for the birthday of Jesus. We have so many fun things to do, parties to go to, and good things to eat. What does this verse mean, though, about God coming to get rid of my enemies? What enemies? Does it mean that Jesus will save me from the monsters that I have nightmares about? Mom tells me I am okay when I wake up screaming from a nightmare. Jesus is guarding me and taking care of me. I wonder what happened to kids before Jesus was born a long time ago. He is now with us to save us from the monster in our nightmares. Thank you, God, for sending Jesus to earth to take care of us and save us from monsters. Amen"

**Do you have nightmares?**

**Isn't it good news to know that Jesus is watching over us?**

## December 2

Psalm 72:6 May the reign of this son of mine be as gentle and fruitful as the springtime rains upon the grass—like showers that water the earth!

Amy was caught up watching the first snowfall of the winter

while listening to this verse. "Here it is snowing, and this verse is about the reign of Jesus being as gentle and fruitful as the springtime rains. The showers water the earth, and the snow is gentle also. The snow is announcing that this gentle person will bring God's love to the people. Jesus will be the springtime rain for the dry, thirsty soul of mankind. He will take away their thirst for truth. Jesus was born to tell us about God, his Father, loving us so very much. We are to come to his Father, trusting like little children. Thank you, Father, for sending your son, Jesus. Amen"

**Has Jesus been like springtime rain for your soul?**

**When did you first experience the love of Jesus?**

# December 3

1 Corinthians 4:5 When the Lord comes, he will turn on the light so that everyone can see exactly what each one of us is really like, deep down in our hearts.

Ted wondered what this verse meant about Jesus turning on the light to show us what is in our hearts. "The Christmas tree lights are so neat. When they are turned on, they show us the peace, joy, and warmth that only he can bring to us. Is he like the Christmas tree lighting up our lives? If we turn to Jesus for his help, for his love and the love of God, his Father, won't our hearts be filled with the colorful lights of Christmas? God sent his Son to show us the way to his peace and joy. Are we willing to accept God's gift of love? I pray that my heart will be bright like a Christmas tree."

**Does your heart have God's peace and joy lighting it up?**

**Is your heart like a Christmas tree?**

# December 4

Psalm 72:7 May all good men flourish in his reign, with abundance of peace to the end of time.

Sara remembered what her religion teacher said the other day. "Mrs. Lewis said that God wants us to live our lives abundantly. He wants to make us whole, complete, and satisfied in his love, joy, and peace. I can imagine the Jewish people waiting for the Messiah to come and save their people. We also are waiting for the birthday of Jesus to arrive to remind all of us that the Messiah did come. He was born. His name is Jesus. He is with us until the end of time. If we will allow him into our hearts, we will feel the abundance of his peace forever. We will feel his peace in our hearts in the midst of heartache and suffering, as well as in joy and laughter. Having Jesus in our hearts enables us to live life abundantly to the fullest. Thank you, God, for the gift of Christmas that is the birthday of Jesus."

**How can you live life to the fullest?**

**What is your wish for Christmas?**

# December 5

Isaiah 40:11 He will feed his flock like a Shepherd; he will carry the lambs in his arms and gently lead the ewes with young.

Sally loved the picture she had showing Jesus carrying a lamb in his arms. "I often imagine myself being that little lamb, feeling safe and warm in the arms of Jesus. I guess Jesus does lead all of us, and if we allow him, he will feed us with his wisdom, love, joy, and peace. But sometimes people, just like lambs, get lost and wander around. Some lambs don't want to find their way back to the flock. Jesus feels so sad that they are lost, even though he tells them he is with them to help them if they will allow him into their lives. Christmas will soon be here, and we will celebrate the birthday of Jesus. Maybe there will be some lost lambs that will see the joy of Christmas and will want to come back to the flock and be fed by Jesus the Good Shepherd."

**What does Jesus the Good Shepherd mean to you?**

**Have you ever felt like a lost lamb?**

# December 6

Psalm 118: 25–26 O Lord, please help us. Save us. Give us success. Blessed is the one who is coming, the one sent by the Lord. We bless you from the temple.

Amy was on the youth group Christmas decorating committee at church. "I don't understand why we can't come up with a decorating scheme we all can agree on. It's so frustrating not being able to come up with some kind of a compromise. After all, this is for Christmas and peace on earth, and here we are bickering with each other about decorations. Actually, our youth group is blessed by having so many creative people as members of the group. I think maybe our own need for control and pride is getting in the way. Who are we putting these decorations together for? Are they for the people in the church to enjoy, or for our own egos to enjoy and take credit for? Yes, God, please help us. Give us success in decorating the church for your birthday and for the Christmas season celebrating your birth. Free us from our prideful egos. Help us to work together for the common good. Amen."

**What does Christmas mean to you?**

**What is your favorite Christmas decoration? Why?**

# December 7

Isaiah 55: 8–9 This plan of mine is not what you would work out, neither are my thoughts the same as yours! For just as the heavens are higher than the earth, so are my ways higher than yours, and my thoughts than yours.

Ted often wondered why a Messiah was needed to save us. "Why did the Messiah come as a little baby? How could a baby save the world? Couldn't God just send a few lightening bolts to zap the people into shape? I guess not. It looks like God doesn't work that way. He seems to prefer giving us a choice to choose his way. He gives us freedom. Yet, he loves us so much that he sent Jesus to be human like us. Jesus felt all of our human emotions and yet, he set a beautiful example of doing his Father's will. Jesus promises to be with us, to lead us, and to help us do his Father's will. I don't understand your plan, God, but I thank you for sending Jesus on that beautiful day of his birth to be the bridge between your ways and our ways. Amen."

**What are the differences between your way of doing things and God's ways?**

**Do you ask God to help you follow his ways?**


# December 8

Isaiah 30:18 Yet the Lord still waits for you to come to him, so he can show you his love; he will conquer you to bless you, just as he said. For the Lord is faithful to his promises. Blessed are all those who wait for him to help them.

Amanda Adams looked at her children as she read this verse to them. "What beautiful children they are, God. I am so grateful for all of your help. How often I come to you asking for your wisdom and guidance in raising them. With the coming of Christmas, I am reminded that another year is ending, and with your birth, a new year is beginning. I always feel renewed at Christmas because I can look back over the year and see the changes and growth that have taken place. The changes that I am not happy with, I put into your care, grateful in knowing that you will carry the load for me. The changes I am happy with, I mentally wrap in boxes and put them under the Christmas tree as treasured gifts. Thank you, God."

**What do you do with your cares and worries?**

**Do you mentally wrap your blessings and put them under the Christmas tree as treasured gifts?**

# December 9

Psalm 103: 1–2 I bless the holy name of God with all my heart. Yes, I will bless the Lord and not forget the glorious things he does for me.

Jim Adams thought about all the glorious things that God had done for him and his family. "It has been a good year, Lord, filled with your many blessings. Things have gone well at work this year. The children have grown, and each has done well in school. Jake will soon be home again from college for his Christmas break. We are so proud of him. Most of all, God, I am so grateful that all the children have grown in their faith and love for you. I can see them turning to you for strength and wisdom. They are living out their faith each and every day. Christmas is such a special time of year. It holds out the gift of your love for those who have lost their way in life. The celebration of your birth, Jesus, is a light in the window of hope extending an invitation to those who are lost. Thank you, God. Amen."

**What blessings have come your way this year?**

**What hopes do you have for the coming year?**

# December 10

Isaiah 35:5 Encourage those who are afraid. Tell them, "Be strong, fear not, for your God is coming to destroy your enemies. He is coming to save you."

Sara wondered what the verse meant when it mentioned "the enemies." "Do I have any enemies? No, I don't think so. What do I have to be afraid of? What do I need God to save me from? I don't know. If any person is my enemy, I don't know about it. I don't believe that God would destroy that person because God loves all people. So what else could be my enemy? Could being afraid be an enemy? It stops me from standing up in class to give a talk. Is my being jealous of someone preventing me from being all I can be? So, is my jealousy an enemy to me? How about my over-blown pride? Is that an enemy to me? The baby Jesus was born to take away our enemies of our own making, which prevent us from being all that we can be in the eyes of God. The baby Jesus gives us encouragement in the form of a tiny baby. How wonderful. Amen."

**Do you have any enemies?**

**What forms of encouragement do you receive from God?**

# December 11

Isaiah 40: 9–10 "Your God is coming!" Yes, the Lord God is coming with mighty power; he will rule with awesome strength.

Ted wasn't too sure about the phrase "awesome strength." "The Jewish people were expecting a warrior God, a fighting God. Yes, they expected a God with awesome strength. When the Messiah came, he came as a helpless baby. He was born into a family that had no worldly power. Jesus worked as a carpenter for a trade. He lived in a quiet village. When he began his ministry, he wasn't accepted by the people of his own village. In the eyes of the world, Jesus ended up a failure. He died on a cross. Yet, in the eyes of God, this Messiah had awesome strength. He had the awesome strength of courage and trust, which carried Jesus on to do God's will. Jesus was to be the bridge that connected man and God through the resurrection. That helpless baby changed the world by bringing the kingdom of God to mankind. I pray for those in the world who do not yet see the awesome strength of God in that baby Jesus."

**What do you feel when you think of Jesus being an infant?**

**What does the phrase "awesome strength" mean to you?**

# December 12

Psalm 144: 1–2 Bless the Lord who is my immovable Rock. He gives me strength and skill in battle. He is always kind and loving to me; he is my fortress, my tower of strength and safety, my deliverer.

Amy went Christmas shopping at the Mall and had a great time. "I love the Christmas season! The shopping Mall was so festive. I found Christmas presents for everyone, so my shopping is done. I need to write some cards and get them in the mail. I think I remembered everyone. Oh, Jesus, I forgot about you. It's your birthday we are celebrating. I realize that exchanging gifts and good will is like doing the same for you, but I need to remember you in a extra special way. How? I guess the best thing I can do for your birthday is to return your gift of love for me. I will be open to your truth and wisdom. I will spend time with you in silence listening for your truth. You want me to do your will, which never changes. You want me to love you with my whole heart, to love my neighbor, and to love myself. You want to share your friendship with me. Amen."

**What are you going to give the Baby Jesus for His birthday?**

**What does God's will mean to you?**

# December 13

Psalm 80:19 Turn us again to yourself, O God of the armies of heaven. Look down on us, your face aglow with joy and love - only then shall we be saved.

Amanda Adams thought about the image of God with his face aglow with joy and love. "God, we do need your help in turning us to you. We humans are so frail. We forget about you in a split second with the slightest distraction. Your birthday is coming up soon, Jesus, and most of us get so caught up in the activities, parties, and preparations of the big day that we entirely forget about you. We forget the meaning of Christmas. Only when we turn to you do we really know what Christmas is all about. We begin to understand just how much you love us by sending us your son to be one of us and to experience first hand what it feels like to be human. Through Jesus, you are turning us again to you. Thank you, God. Amen."

**What are some of the things of Christmas that turn your heart aglow with joy and love?**

**Are you able to keep focused on what Christmas really means?**

# December 14

Psalm 25:8 The Lord is good and glad to teach the proper path to all who go astray; he will teach the ways that are right and best to those who humbly turn to him.

Sally was really getting excited about the holidays. "I wish I had been alive when Jesus was a little boy. Wouldn't it be fun going to a birthday party for Jesus? I wonder what kind of a little boy he was. I wonder if he ever had a birthday party. I bet he did. What would he say to me? He would have been a good friend and watch that I didn't hurt myself? Gosh, he does that now. Jesus teaches me right from wrong. Even though Jesus hasn't lived on earth for a very long time, we have Christmas so that we will be reminded each year about how much God loves us. So once again I am making plans for celebrating Jesus' birthday. What will I give him for his birthday? What would he like? I know; he wants me to love him and care about everyone in the world. He wants me to be kind to those around me and to be thoughtful to my family. What a wonderful gift!"

**What would you like to give Jesus for his birthday?**

**What are your favorite Christmas gifts to receive?**

# December 15

Psalm 34: 4–5 For I cried to him and he answered me! He freed me from all my fears. Others too were radiant at what he did for them. Theirs was no downcast look of rejection!

Amanda Adams remembered back when she felt fear. She was filled with all kinds of worries and anxieties. "I don't know exactly when it happened, but over a period of time, I came to the realization that God loved me and was with me. It was a slow process, but I continued to cry to God for his peace. In so doing, I became more relaxed and less fearful. I realized that all was well. No matter what happens in our lives, all will be well. So I look forward to Christmas Day, which celebrates the beginning of Jesus bridging the gap between us and God. The birth of Jesus is a sign that all will be well. Do I have the real faith to believe that? With God's help, I believe it. It is a mystery. The older I get, the more I realize that I don't know much. So it's for me to accept God's mysteries. Thank you, God. All is well. Amen."

**Are you able to accept God's mysteries?**

**Do you believe that all will be well?**


# December 16

Isaiah 49:13 Sing a song for joy, O heavens; shout, O earth. Break forth with song, O mountains, for the Lord has comforted his people, and will have compassion upon them in their sorrow.

Sara decided that she wanted to give her friends Christmas cards. "I never thought about giving out cards before, so this is a new experience for me. I think I will make my own out of construction paper. I feel so happy that I want to share my happiness with others. By making my own cards, I can tell them how much they mean to me. God has been so good to me. When I turn to him when I feel sad, it seems that a feeling of peace comes over me. God shows his love for me in many different ways. I want to show my love for others, and making my own Christmas cards will be a great way of expressing myself. I will make a birthday card for you, Jesus, and hang it on the Christmas tree. Yes, God, I feel like singing for joy. Happy birthday!"

**What makes you want to sing for joy?**

**In what ways has God comforted you?**

# December 17

Haggai 2: 8–9 "The future splendor of this Temple will be greater than the splendor of the first one! For I have plenty of silver and gold to do it! And here I will give peace, says the Lord."

Jake was glad to be back home from college. "Home is a temple for me. My roots are here. I know that I will move on to a future temple, and I pray that my future temple will be at least as great as this one. I'm sure the temple that the Jewish people once had was a symbol of their roots. They wanted a future temple that was greater than the first. Little did they realize that the future temple would be found in the person of Jesus Christ. The temple was not in a building, but instead in a man; the Son of God. Jesus Christ is God's gift of peace. Christmas shines forth each year in a splendor of tinsel, bright lights, ornaments, and joyful songs. What a beautiful temple we have in Jesus. He is our rock. He is our foundation. Thank you, God, for the gift of your Son. Amen."

**What type of temple are you looking for?**

**Will you find peace in this future temple?**

# December 18

Matthew 1:23 "Listen! The virgin shall conceive a child! She shall give birth to a Son, and he shall be called 'Emanuel'(meaning 'God is with us')."

Sally was so excited. "We are going to decorate the Christmas tree this evening. I can hardly wait! It is all I can do to sit still. I wish this prayer would end pretty soon. I want to get started. Oh, I think I have gotten off on the wrong track. I'm sorry, God. The most important thing for me to do is to take time out to sit quietly with you. You are Emanuel, and you are with us. As we trim the tree in your honor, you are there and enjoying the fun right along with us. It takes this time of quiet to settle myself down to listen to you. I need to remind myself that we are decorating the tree to celebrate your birthday. Let's have fun. Amen."

**What is your favorite way to celebrate your birthday?**

**What was your favorite birthday?**

# December 19

Psalm 71: 5–6 O Lord, you alone are my hope; I've trusted you from childhood. Yes, you have been with me from birth and have helped me constantly—no wonder I am always praising you!

Jim Adams agreed with this verse deep in his heart. "Yes, Lord, you have been at my side all of my life. There were times when I never thought about you. I thought it was through my own abilities that the good things in life happened. I didn't give you the credit. I learned, though, during the down times when things weren't going well, that I had no power on my own to change things. I realized that I needed your help. Some things couldn't be changed, but through the trial, you gave me a peace of heart to get through it and to grow from the situation. I find that Christmas is a wonderful way to express my praise and thanks to you. The tree we trimmed shouts for joy in its splendor. Yes, God, you are my hope. I've learned that I can indeed trust you. Thank you. Amen."

**Is your heart trimmed like a beautiful Christmas tree?**

**Does your heart shout for joy?**

# December 20

Luke 1:78–79 All this will be because the mercy of our God is very tender, and heaven's dawn is about to break upon us, to give light to those who sit in darkness and death's shadow, and to guide us to the path of peace.

Amy wrapped all of her presents to put under the tree. "I hope they will like what I bought them. I didn't have very much money to spend, but I did put a lot of thought into what I bought. I wanted to show my family that I really do love them. Oh, I forgot to get a present to give to Jesus. What do you suppose he would like? I know that the greatest gift for me to give to Jesus is my love. How can I wrap that up into a present to put under the tree? The other day I was asked to join a youth bible group at church. I said I would think about it. Jesus, what I will do is writing in a Christmas card that I will join the study group. I'll put the card in a box and wrap it and place it under the tree. My gift to you, Jesus, is to learn about your word so that I can get closer to you."

**Have you ever felt like you are in darkness?**

**When did the mercy of God break through?**

# December 21

Psalm 33: 21–22 No wonder we are happy in the Lord! For we are trusting him. We trust his holy name. Yes, Lord, let your constant love surround us, for our hopes are in you alone.

Ted was going out with a group of kids from church to sing Christmas carols one evening. "I enjoy singing. The Christmas carols are my favorite songs. At first when I was little, the carols seemed like nice stories about little Jesus, about lambs, shepherds, stars, and wise men. It didn't really make much sense to me. Then one day I began realizing that this nice Christmas story about the birth of Jesus was a testimony of God's love for us. He sent this innocent baby Jesus into the world as one of us to experience life with us and to love us. Jesus promised never to abandon us. He is one with us. He is standing at the door, waiting for us to open it and let him in. All we need to do is answer his knock on the door of our hearts. He will then enter our hearts."

**What are your favorite Christmas carols?**

**What do the words mean to you?**

# December 22

Isaiah 9:6 For unto us a child is born; unto us a Son is given; and the government shall be upon his shoulders. These will be his royal titles: "Wonderful," "Counselor," "The Mighty God." "The Everlasting Father," "The Prince of Peace."

Amanda Adams had felt sad most of the day. She was thinking about the Christmas party they attended the night before. "The party was beautiful. It was filled with good food, music, and company. Then I saw the couple who suffered the loss of a close relative last month. My heart ached for them. They were trying so hard to be of good cheer but I am sure the happiness all around them made their loss hurt even more. I pray that Jesus will shoulder their grief and pain for them. He will be the Prince of Peace to them and bring his peace into their hearts. I guess it is time for me to hand the sadness I have been feeling up to you, dear Counselor. I am not helping anyone by feeling sad. Instead, I now turn my sadness into a prayer for all the hurting people in the world."

**What is your favorite title for God?**

**Are you able to place your problems on God's shoulders?**

# December 23

Galatians 4:4 But when the right time came the time God decided on, he sent his Son, born of a woman, born as a Jew, to buy freedom for us who were slaves to the law so that he could adopt us as his very own sons.

Jake had been busy seeing his high school friends who were home from college, so he hadn't thought much about the meaning of Christmas. "Boy, I have really been on the go since I got home. There is another party tonight, and I think my family is starting to feel like I am ignoring them. Do you feel that way also, God? I'll admit I have had a great time seeing everyone. It has been relaxing after all the months of studying. Yet, I guess I'd better keep things in balance. I know you and my family want me to relax and have fun. They just want me to spend a little time with them. You want the same thing, only you go everywhere with me. All I need to do is to acknowledge that you are with me. I've been pretty self-centered. I'm sorry, God. I'll be more thoughtful from now on. I know that you are with me."

**Have you ever become self-centered at Christmas time?**

**What were the results of you being self-centered?**

# December 24

Luke 2: 6–7 And while they were there, the time came for her baby to be born; and she gave birth to her first child; a son. She wrapped him in a blanket and laid him in a manger, because there was no room for them in the village inn.

Ted had to admit he was feeling pretty happy." I know it isn't cool for a guy my age to feel excited about Christmas, but it is pretty neat to be a member of this family spending Christmas Eve together. The tree looks fantastic, and the presents are overflowing. The phone has rung off the hook with calls from friends and relatives. We guys got together this afternoon and played some basketball. It's been a really neat day. I'm looking forward to going to the Christmas service at church later tonight. Jesus, how did you celebrate your birthday as a guy my age? I remember the story that when you were twelve years old, you sat for three days in Jerusalem talking to the teachers of the Law. Did you ever play sports in Nazareth, Jesus?

**What kind of a baby do you think Jesus was?**

**What kind of a baby were you?**

# December 25

Luke 2:10–11 But the angel reassured them. "Don't be afraid!" he said. "I bring you the most joyful news ever announced, and it is for everyone! The Savior—yes, the Messiah, the Lord—has been born tonight in Bethlehem!

Sally was enjoying every minute of the day of Christmas. "Jesus, I have had the nicest time celebrating your birthday. We went to church last night and then opened our presents this morning. I loved every present I received. And now here we are, Jesus, with you at the dinner table. Mom decorated the dining room with red and green streamers and balloons, just like I asked her to. The birthday cake she baked for you is sitting in the middle of the table. We will eat it right after this quiet time in prayer with you. What do you want me to give to you for your birthday? I know—you want my love, my trust, and my heart. You want my friendship. Here is my heart, Jesus. Happy birthday!"

**What are your Christmas traditions?**

**Are you able to give Jesus your heart, your love, and your trust?**


# December 26

Luke 2:18–19 All who heard the shepherds' story expressed astonishment, but Mary quietly treasured these things in her heart and often thought about them.

Amanda Adams thought about Mary. "What a beautiful example of love and trust is found in Mary. She accepted the role of being the mother of Jesus. She must have been confused at times, but she freely accepted the mystery and surrendered to God's will. Her heart must have been filled with joy as she held her beautiful baby son. She was away from her mother and her relatives in this town of Bethlehem. She and Joseph must have missed the warm ties of their families being with them to share the joy. Yet, there were the shepherds who stopped by. There were the Wisemen who came to see this holy child. This child's birth was to be celebrated not only by his immediate family, but by the whole world as well."

**What do you think Mary thought about as she held her son?**

**What do you think the shepherds thought?**


# December 27

Matthew 2: 9–10 After this interview the astrologers started out again. And look! The star appeared to them again, standing over Bethlehem. Their joy knew no bounds!

Sally remembered seeing pictures of the three Wisemen. "We have the three Wisemen with our nativity set also. I love to look at the nativity set, which we put under our Christmas tree every year. It must have been wonderful to be there with the shepherds and the Wisemen. I bet the star was so bright. I wonder if it lit up the night sky so much that it made shadows like the full moon does. I wonder what baby Jesus looked like. I bet he was a pretty baby. Mary and Joseph must have felt so happy. I'm always a bit sad when Christmas is over. Next week, we all go back to school and real life begins again. Each Christmas I learn more about Jesus, and I carry what I've learned into real life. Thank you, God. Amen."

**What do you learn each Christmas?**

**What do you carry from Christmas into the real life each year?**

# December 28

Matthew 2:11 Entering the house where the baby and Mary his mother were, they threw themselves down before him, worshiping. Then they opened their presents and gave him gold, frankincense and myrrh.

Jake was thinking about going back to school in a few days, so his mind was wandering. "I've had a great time being at home and seeing my old friends, yet I'm looking forward to going back to college and being with my friends there. I guess this is a time of change for me. Although it was hard for me at first, I am enjoying it all very much now. The birth of Jesus was the beginning of a change for mankind, wasn't it? How fortunate the Wisemen were to recognize the change and accept it with open arms—to recognize Jesus, give him presents, and worship him. I wonder how I would have reacted if I had lived then and had seen the star? Would I have recognized the change?

**If you had lived back in the time when Jess was born, would you have followed the star?**

**Do you follow the star today?**

# December 29

John 1:14 And Christ became a human being and lived here on earth among us and was full of loving forgiveness and truth.

Sally wondered what it would be like if Jesus was alive today. "What if Jesus moved in next door and was my age? He would be in the first grade like I am. I wonder what he would look like. I bet Mary and Joseph would be friends of my mom and dad. Would Joseph work in his yard like Dad does? Would Jesus help his dad? Would he take the trash outside for Mary like I do for Mom? I wonder if he would have a cat and a dog for a pet. Would Mary and Joseph give Jesus a birthday party and invite all of his friends? Would I be a friend? If I were invited, what would I give to Jesus? I think I would make him something. But what? I guess all I have to give him is myself. He wants my friendship. I would make a birthday card for Jesus saying 'I love you, Jesus.' That's what I would do."

**What kind off a birthday present would you give to Jesus?**

**If you made him a birthday card, what would it say?**

# December 30

John 3:16–17 "For God loved the world so much that he gave his only Son so that anyone who believes in him shall not perish but have eternal life. God did not send his Son into the world to condemn it, but to save it."

Jim Adams nodded his head in agreement. "The New Year is nearing, and the joys of the Christmas season will once again fade into memory. What we forget, though, is that Christmas is the acknowledgment and celebration of Jesus' birthday. It illustrates how very much God loves us. Sometimes I think many of us believe that Jesus was sent into the world to condemn it. How many rules and regulations do people try to hold over our heads in the name of Jesus? Don't do this. Don't do that. Don't break the rules or you will be damned. God didn't send his Son into the world to condemn it. He sent Jesus into the world to save us, to help us live life abundantly, and to help us become free from the slavery of sin. Thank you, Father, for your love. Amen."

**Do you believe that God loves you so much that he sent his Son into the world to save you?**

**In what ways has God helped you?**

# December 31

Luke 2:21 Eight days later, at the baby's circumcision ceremony, he was named Jesus, the name give him by the angel before he was even conceived.

Amanda Adams felt happy and content. "This has been a good year for our family. Our scripture reading and silent reflection after dinner has been very helpful. I'm so glad our family has been so enthused about it. It has indeed become a family tradition. Each of us has grown closer to you, God. I pray that the coming New Year will be filled with your wonderful blessings. I thank you, God, for this grace-filled year we will be leaving behind at midnight. Happy New Year!"

**What blessings has God given to you this year?**

**What are you most grateful for?**

# New Year's Day

Hebrews 10:16 "I will write my laws into their *minds* so that they will always know my will, and I will put my laws in their *hearts* so that they will want to obey them."

Amanda Adams remembered back when she first learned about God. "The Ten Commandments were very important to me. I had it drilled into my head about what was good and what was bad. One day, after having gone through some pretty down times, I realized just how much I needed God. As time went on, I realized just how much I loved God. The laws were drilled into my *mind* so that I would know his will. Through God's grace the laws became apart of my *heart.* I now want to obey his will because I love God so much. Thank you for your grace of love. Amen."

**Do you know the laws and God's will?**

**Have the laws become a part of your *heart*?**

TATE PUBLISHING *& Enterprises*

Tate Publishing is commited to excellence in the publishing industry. Our staff of hightly trained professionals, including editors, graphic designers, and marketing personnel, work together to produce the very finest books available. The company reflects the philosophy established by the founders, based on Psalms 68:11,

"THE LORD GAVE THE WORD AND GREAT WAS THE COMPANY OF THOSE WHO PUBLISHED IT."

If you would like further information, please call
1.888.361.9473
or visit our website
www.tatepublishing.com

TATE PUBLISHING *& Enterprises*, LLC
127 E. Trade Center Terrace
Mustang, Oklahoma 73064 USA

61719158R00153

Made in the USA
Lexington, KY
18 March 2017